LET'S-TALK-ABOUT-IT STORIES FOR KIDS

Thanks for Being My Friend

LOIS WALFRID JOHNSON

Illustrations by Virginia Peck

NAVPRESS

A MINISTRY OF THE NAVIGATORS

P.O. BOX 6000, COLORADO SPRINGS, COLORADO 80934

The Navigators is an international Christian organization. Jesus Christ gave His followers the Great Commission to go and make disciples (Matthew 28:19). The aim of The Navigators is to help fulfill that commission by multiplying laborers for Christ in every nation.

NavPress is the publishing ministry of The Navigators. NavPress publications are tools to help Christians grow. Although publications alone cannot make disciples or change lives, they can help believers learn biblical discipleship, and apply what they learn to their lives and ministries.

CONTENTS

To all the Ericksons—
Hope and Leighton,
Anna Lisa, Alycia, and Iantha—
friends I can count on.

AUTHOR

When Lois Walfrid Johnson was nine years old she wondered, "What do I want to be when I grow up?" She sensed God's call to be a writer. If she could possibly write a book, she wanted to tell others what she believed about Jesus Christ.

That desire stayed with her through high school, college, and the early years of her marriage to Roy Johnson, an elementary school teacher. When the youngest of their three children entered first grade, Lois became a full-time free-lance writer. Her articles, poetry, and books have been published in English-speaking countries throughout the world and translated into nine languages.

Lois Johnson is the author of thirteen books,

including *Secrets of the Best Choice, You're Worth More Than You Think!,* and *You Are Wonderfully Made!* in the *LET'S-TALK-ABOUT-IT* series. She has also written *Just a Minute, Lord* and *You're My Best Friend, Lord* for pre-teens; *Come as You Are* for young teens; *Gift in My Arms, Either Way, I Win,* and *Falling Apart or Coming Together* for adults. Lois leads seminars and retreats and speaks at churches and conferences throughout the United States.

ACKNOWLEDGMENTS

With gratitude to Jesus Christ, my most important relationship, and warm thanks to these other valued people in my life: Kathy Boyum, Diane Brask, Larry Hackett, Judy Hinchey, Jeffrey Johnson, Kevin Johnson, and Beverly Sandberg for background information; Traci Mullins, Jerry Foley, Charette Kvernstoen, Penny Stokes, and Terry White for help with the manuscript; my husband, Roy, for the love, wisdom, and daily caring out of which good relationships are built.

TO KIDS WHO READ THIS BOOK

"I wish I could be more popular with the other kids," said Jenny.

Do you have the same wish? Or do you think of it another way? "I'd like to be a sports hero—or a TV star—or an astronaut."

Eric was afraid to tell what he'd like to be. But he spent every spare minute throwing a football. Someday, maybe, he'd make the long pass that would win a big game. And wow! What a day that would be!

If you have those secret feelings, you have plenty of company. Most of us want people to admire what we do. We want them to think we're great! We'd like to have them cheering for us.

Feeling that way can help you make good choices:

11

being more thoughtful of others, working hard to succeed, choosing right actions instead of wrong.

But when Jenny said, "I want to be more popular," and when Eric practiced football, they were saying more: "I want to be loved. I want to be noticed. I want to have friends."

Friends come in all sizes and shapes. Some are young, some old, some just your age. Some are members of your family, relatives, neighbors, or pets. Some are kids next door, at church, or at school.

Friends are kids and grownups you know and love. They're people you have fun with and people who cry with you when you hurt.

The stories in this book are about kids who want friends. They want good relationships with others. But these kids don't always have it easy. Sometimes they're mad, or afraid, or mixed-up. Sometimes they feel everyone else wins. Sometimes they think, "I don't have a friend in the world." And often they find that in their relationships they need to make choices.

Maybe they're facing problems like yours. Or problems like those of someone who lived a long time ago.

The Bible tells about a man named Daniel who was a prisoner of war living in Babylon. Daniel's king liked him and wanted to make him ruler over the whole kingdom. But Daniel's enemies plotted against him. They asked the king to issue a command that no one could pray to any god or man except the king.

Daniel had to make a choice. Would he try to do what was popular? Would he do what others wanted, even though it was wrong? Or would he choose God's way, no matter what the cost?

Daniel's life was at stake, but he didn't try to hide his choice. He threw open his windows toward Jerusalem. Three times a day he prayed to the Lord God of Israel, asking for help.

His enemies told the king, and Daniel was thrown into the lion's den. All night long, man-eating lions surrounded him. But in the morning, Daniel was unharmed. No wound was found on him because he trusted in his God.

In the choices you need to make, you can be like Daniel and ask God for help. And, as you read this book, you can help the kids in the stories make choices. Talk about the questions. Think of ways to solve the problems they face. Think of ways to solve your own problems.

Then turn the book upside down. Repeat the Bible verse to yourself until you receive the help it gives. Read the prayer, or pray one of your own. Whenever you turn to God, you receive a power greater than your own.

If you're thinking, "I want friends who like me," there's Someone named Jesus who does more than that. Whoever you are, He *loves* you. He cheers you on.

He stands ready, holding His arms open, always ready to help.

With Him you can say, *Thanks for Being My Friend.*

SATURDAY MORNING CARWASH

That evening the kids from church started talking about how to raise money. Sherri, one of the girls in their Sunday school class, needed a kidney transplant. Her family needed money for medical bills.

Libby took charge. She liked organizing things and asked for ideas on what to do.

"We could have a pancake supper," suggested one girl. "Our moms and dads would help."

"How about a dash for trash?" asked a boy. "People could sponsor us, and we'd clean up cans and other trash along roads."

Finally they decided to hold a carwash on a Saturday morning two weeks away.

"My dad will let us have it in the bank parking lot," said Libby's best friend, Pam. "It's on a busy corner and lots of people will see us."

"Great!" said Libby. "Let's make a list of what we need. First, someone for publicity. Who's good at posters?"

"I am," said Pam. "I'll put 'em in the stores around here."

"And how about a notice in the church bulletin?" Someone else volunteered.

"Rags and buckets?" Three of the boys offered to bring those.

"Car wax?" A fourth boy said he'd try for a discount at a nearby store.

"Well, that's just about it," said Libby. Then as the group started to break up, she remembered. "We'll need two long hoses or three shorter ones to reach from the outside faucet to the parking lot."

"I'll bring 'em," said Chuck. "We've got two long hoses."

"Terrific," answered Libby. "Now, does everyone know what they're supposed to do?"

Picking up the list, she read off each person's job. "Then we're all set. Talk about the carwash wherever you are. The more customers we get, the more money we'll make for Sherri. And everyone be there at 8:45."

The Saturday of the carwash dawned warm and sunny. As the kids gathered at the parking lot, Libby

16

knew the girls had done a great job on publicity. Wherever she went, people promised they'd show up. Now, fifteen minutes before the carwash was to start, she checked to be sure they had everything.

"Buckets? Rags? Wax? Yep. And plenty of kids to help." Libby was pleased.

But the next minute she felt a jolt. "Where's Chuck with the two hoses?"

No one had seen Chuck that morning. "Oh-oh, are we in trouble?" asked Libby, her heart starting to pound.

"I'll go call," said Pam. But the bank was locked. The nearest outside phone was a block away.

Just then their first customer drove in. A moment later three other cars lined up back of the first. Libby looked at them, glad for the business. "But oh, wow! How can we keep up without a hose?"

She sent three of the boys with buckets to the faucet. But the cars were too dirty. Soon muddy brown water filled each bucket.

Libby felt frantic. "We're gonna lose customers," she said, trying to set up a bucket brigade.

She was right. The driver of the third car gave a quick beep. Libby went over to explain what was wrong. He pulled out of line and drove off.

The driver of the fourth car got out. "Hey, what's the trouble? Can I help?"

Libby felt relieved when she recognized Mr.

17

Morris, a man from their church.

"I've got two short hoses," he said. "I live three miles from here, but I'll see what else I can round up." Starting his car, he hurried away.

Just then another driver pulled in. When Libby explained, the woman said, "Sorry, I wanted to help out. But I can't wait around all day."

The man in the next car felt the same way and left.

Libby didn't blame them, but she felt more angry every minute. Each customer they lost meant less money for Sherri. "All that publicity wasted. . . ."

But Libby also felt embarrassed. It hurt to plan something and not have it work. "I wonder if people think it's my fault?" She dreaded seeing another customer—someone who'd think she didn't know what she was doing.

Just then Chuck rode up on his bike. Libby pounced on him. "Where are the hoses?"

"Hoses?" Chuck looked blank, then remembered. "Ohhh. I forgot."

"You *forgot*?" asked Libby. "The whole carwash depends on you, and you *forgot*?"

She couldn't remember ever being so mad. Picking up a bucket, she dumped the muddy water over Chuck's head. "You sure are dumb!"

As Chuck sputtered, Libby picked up another bucket and stomped over to a waiting car. "How long before Mr. Morris comes back?" she wondered.

18

TO TALK ABOUT

▶Being responsible means being someone others can count on. How did everyone except Chuck accept responsibility?

▶What does it mean to say, "A chain is only as strong as its weakest link"? Who was the weakest link? How did all the kids suffer because he forgot his part?

▶Why is it important that Libby told Chuck how she felt?

▶Did Libby have a right to be angry about the hoses? Why or why not? When was Jesus angry about things people did? (See Mark 3:1-5 and John 2:13-17 for clues.) Do these verses mean Libby has a right to be angry whenever she feels like it? Why or why not?

▶Does Libby have a right to hold a grudge toward Chuck? Why or why not?

▶When the carwash is over and Libby cools down, she needs to talk more with Chuck. Instead of saying, "*You* sure are dumb!" she could find a better way of expressing how she feels. She might say, "*I'm* mad because we didn't have the hose when we needed it." How would that make a difference in how Chuck feels?

▶What does Chuck need to do to set things right?

▶Is there something that makes you angry? How do you need to deal with it?

19

If someone has done you a wrong, do not repay him with a wrong. Try to do what everyone considers to be good. (Romans 12:17, GNB)

Jesus, when I feel mad, help me handle it in the right way. Help me talk to the person I have a problem with. Help me forgive that person and put the problem behind me.

CAMP SHOWOFF

Rick swung onto the upper bunk and lay down. From there he watched Jeff, his counselor. When Jeff wasn't looking, Rick slid into his sleeping bag with all his clothes still on.

He'd been at church camp for two days now. They hadn't been easy days. Already the camp director had gotten after Rick for throwing food in the dining hall. Even worse, Rick felt strange about being with these kids. Sure, he liked Jeff. And Paul and some of the other guys in his cabin were great.

But Rick wished he could belong. He always felt at the edge of things. For some reason he needed to prove himself.

Now it haunted him. "I didn't want to be rude to

Paul, but I was." Earlier that day Paul started talking about the neat things he and his dad did together. Next week Paul's family would go on a trip.

Hearing about it, Rick blurted out, "Aw, my dad's got a better job than yours. He's gonna take me on a trip to Hawaii."

Paul looked kind of strange, but didn't say anything. He didn't say anything more about his own family either.

"Maybe he knows I only see Dad once a year," thought Rick. "Maybe he knows Dad won't take me to Hawaii."

Suddenly Rick felt ashamed about the lie and about trying to look good. At the same time he thought, "I'll show 'em. I'll get 'em to notice me." He thought about the big plans he'd made.

"Good night, everyone!" called out Jeff, as he turned out the lights. Rick lay in the darkness, going through his plans step by step. "All I've gotta do is wait until everyone's asleep."

The minutes ticked away and Rick grew restless. The other boys talked and joked and finally grew quiet. At last Rick dared to lean down, trying to peer through the darkness. Even Jeff seemed asleep.

Slowly, carefully, Rick climbed down from the bunk and tiptoed across the room. He even managed to open and close the door without making it squeak. Once outside, he hurried to the place under the cabin where he'd hidden the things he collected.

It took two trips to bring all of it up near the dining hall. Once there, Rick stepped into the flower bed, stood a long, pointed pole upright, and pushed it into the dirt. Taking shorter poles and a rope, he tied two crosspieces into an "X." Then he tied the "X" onto the tall pole.

A yard light gave just enough of a glow for Rick to see how it looked. Standing back to view his work, he felt good. "Yep, it'll make a great scarecrow."

Using jeans for legs and a shirt for arms, he stuffed them with crumpled newspapers he'd found in the trash bin. Then came his masterpiece. Working quickly, Rick filled a pillowcase with more newspapers. Using another piece of rope, he tied the head in place.

Once again Rick stood back. Even in the dim light he saw the face he'd drawn on the pillowcase. Dark hair, glaring eyes, moustache and beard. The mouth turned down in a scowl. The head looked just like Mr. Anderson, the camp director.

Rick grinned. "Just how he looked when he was mad at me."

The next morning the whole camp buzzed. When the rumor started that Rick had done it, he felt good. But no one could prove anything. By afternoon Rick wished he'd left just one clue so he could get credit.

At supper Rick caught his counselor watching

him from across the table. There was something in Jeff's eyes that Rick didn't like. "Can he see right through me?" Rick wondered.

When Thursday night came, everyone gathered at the beach for the closing campfire. Rick sat on the outer edge of the circle, feeling as alone as he had all week. "What a bunch of junk they're dishing out," he thought. "This Jesus—what a friend *He'd* be."

But Rick's heart started to pound, as though it were going to beat right out of his chest. Jeff was speaking to the group that night, and he seemed to be talking right to Rick.

"Are you lonely?" Jeff asked. "There's no one who can fill every space in your heart except Jesus. Are you afraid no one will notice you? Do you lie and show off to get attention? Do you feel like you want to belong, but you're afraid to try? There's one big answer. It's Jesus."

Deep inside, Rick felt like he was crying and couldn't stop. "Sissy stuff," he thought. "I'm not gonna cry for anything."

Pushing down the feeling, Rick thought about leaving. He wanted to run away from the quiet voice telling him about Jesus. He didn't want to be honest in front of the kids. He didn't want to be honest with this Jesus who made him feel uncomfortable.

But Jeff kept talking. "Jesus loves you so much that He died on the cross for you. He died to take away your sin. He loves you. He wants to forgive you. All you have to do is ask Him."

Suddenly Rick couldn't hold it in any longer. He began sobbing and couldn't stop. All the loneliness he'd felt, all the bragging and asking for attention, all the feelings of not fitting in. . . .

When Jeff finished speaking, Rick moved closer to the campfire. "I don't want to tell Jeff what's wrong," thought Rick. But when he did, Jeff told Rick how to ask Jesus for forgiveness.

"And Jesus, I want You to be my Savior and Lord," Rick prayed, the way Jeff told him.

In that moment a great weight fell away from Rick. He drew a deep breath, hardly able to believe it himself. "Jesus loves me," he thought, repeating the words Jeff had told him. "Jesus loves me!"

Inside, he knew it was real.

TO TALK ABOUT

▶Rick wanted to be loved and accepted by the other kids. Even if he knew he belonged, would that take care of all of his emptiness? Why or why not?

▶How do you know Jesus loves Rick very much?

▶Why is Jesus the only Person able to fill the emptiness Rick felt? Why is Jesus the only Person who can help you with *every* need?

▶If you put Jesus first, how will He help you with

your other friendships?

▶Do you know for sure that Jesus is your Savior and Lord? If not, what choice do you need to make?

Jesus said, "Greater love has no one than this, that he lay down his life for his friends." (John 15:13)

If you'd like to invite Jesus into your life, you can pray these words:

Thank You, Jesus, for loving me so much that You died on the cross for me. I'm sorry about my sins, and ask You to forgive me. I ask You to be my Savior and Lord. Thank You for Your salvation!

The Bible promises that "whoever believes in the Son has eternal life" (John 3:36). If you have asked forgiveness for your sin and asked Jesus to be your Lord and Savior, you have eternal life—a life with Jesus on earth and in Heaven forever. It begins right now!

IT'S NOT FAIR!

Tina was mad when she came to the supper table. Partway through the meal, she started in. "You always let Karrin do what she wants. Why does she get to go to the volleyball tournament, and I don't?"

"She's older than you," said Dad. "When you're Karrin's age, you'll get to do the things she's doing now."

But Tina wasn't satisfied. "You and Mom treat her different than you treat me. And you treat Bobby different, too. No matter what he does, you think it's cute."

Dad sighed. "Tina, you know that Karrin is four years older than you, and Bobby is five years younger.

27

We can't possibly treat you all the same."

"It's not fair!" said Tina. "I think you *should* treat us all the same."

"Do you really?" asked Dad. "Do you want a baby-sitter like Bobby has when we go out?"

"Well, no," said Tina. "But he always gets the prize in the cereal box."

Dad laughed. "Are you sure you want those prizes? A lot of them are for four- or five-year-olds. Or do you want the prizes because Bobby wants them?"

"Just the same, it's not fair!"

"Some things aren't fair," said Dad. "Sometimes we need to treat each of you differently. It's not because we love one of you more than another. We try to do what's best for each of you."

For a moment Tina was quiet. "Is that really true?" she wondered. "Do Dad and Mom *really* try to do what's best for each of us?"

Mom broke into her thoughts. "How many for apple pie? There's a little bit left over from last night."

Everyone was too full, except for Karrin and Tina. "I'll cut it," said Tina. "Karrin always takes more than her share."

"Go ahead," said Mom. "You cut it, but then Karrin gets first choice."

Tina groaned, making sure everyone heard. Ever since Tina was a little kid, she'd always hated that rule. If she didn't try to cut something even, she never

28

got a chance to have the biggest piece.

While eating her pie, Tina started thinking again. "Do Mom and Dad really love me as much as Karrin and Bobby? They always seem to get more attention. They always get the best."

Just then the phone rang. Karrin jumped up. When she returned to the table, her face glowed. "David said he'd give me a ride to the game. Okay?"

Mom looked at Dad. "Okay," they said, almost together.

A minute later Karrin was back. "I need to leave in twenty minutes. Can I be excused to get ready?"

Tina exploded. "It's her turn to do dishes!"

"I know it is," said Karrin. "Can you help me out?"

"That's just what I've been talking about. You always get to do stuff I can't do!"

"How about trading with me? I'll do one of your nights next week," said Karrin. "Okay?"

Tina sighed. "Nope. If I do dishes tonight, you work *two* nights for me next week."

"Uh, uh, uh," said Dad. "That's not fair to Karrin!"

Tina looked at Dad. He was right, of course. It wasn't fair. Much as she wanted to take advantage of Karrin, she'd better not—at least not in front of Mom and Dad.

"Okaaay," Tina said, still sounding unhappy with the deal. "I'll do 'em tonight."

Karrin hugged her. "I'll tell you everything about

it when I get home!" she said excitedly.

It seemed forever before Tina finished the dishes. All the way through the glasses and silverware, she felt mad. No matter what Dad said, she still felt Karrin and Bobby got the best end of every deal.

But then as she washed the plates, Tina remembered something—a time when Karrin had helped her out. One of Karrin's friends had three tickets for the ice follies, and Karrin got Tina invited.

As she reached the pots and pans, Tina remembered something else. Once she got to go to the circus with Bobby and his friends. Sure they were younger, but. . . .

By the time Tina wiped off the table and counter, she felt a bit better inside.

She'd been sleeping a couple of hours when her sister crept into their bedroom. As Karrin stumbled over the clothes on the floor, she crashed into a chair. Tina woke up.

She moaned, and Karrin exclaimed, "Oh, I'm so glad you're awake! I want to tell you everything we did."

Karrin turned on the light. Rubbing the sleep out of her eyes, Tina rolled over and stuffed a pillow under her head.

Karrin's face glowed again. "David is so fun! Thanks for doing the dishes so I could get ready!"

As Karrin dropped down on her bed, Tina felt the

cold outside air still clinging to her sister's clothes. But inside Tina felt warm. For the first time in many weeks she wanted to hear Karrin's good news.

TO TALK ABOUT

▶What is a happy family? Is it one where there are never disagreements? Or one where everyone knows it's okay to talk about what bothers them? Why do you think so?

▶Why is it important that Tina talked about how she felt? Do you agree or disagree with the answers Dad gave? Why?

▶What does it mean to compete? Tina was competing for something. What was it? What feeling made her want to compete?

▶In some families everyone competes with everyone else. In others, members of the family try to cooperate. What does it mean to cooperate? How did Tina and Karrin cooperate?

▶Which kind of family is stronger—the one that competes or the one that cooperates? Why?

▶Your father or mother may not live with you. The rules for that house may be different from the house where you live most of the time. Yet you still need to know how to cooperate. How can you work together when you go there?

Don't just think about your own affairs, but be interested in others, too, and in what they are doing.
(Philippians 2:4, TLB)

Jesus, I'm used to looking out for Number One—and that's me. But I want to start thinking about others. Help me learn how to cooperate with my family. Help me care about them.

32

THE OLD
BIKE TRAIL

Jerry felt glad that some-
day his teeth would look better. Yet for now he hated
wearing braces.

"When we're done, you'll have a nice smile," the
dentist had said.

"Someday," thought Jerry. Someday seemed like
forever. It was years away. This morning was *now*—
his first Sunday school class after getting braces. The
bands and wires seemed to fill his entire mouth.

To make matters worse, a new girl joined their
class that day. "Laura looks like fun," thought Jerry.
But then he wondered, "What'll she think of the way I
look?" Leaning his elbow on the table, he covered his
mouth with his hand.

The first time his teacher called on him, Jerry was still thinking about his braces.

"Jerry," said Mrs. Lynden again.

Jerry jumped, as though he just woke up. Everyone laughed.

When he tried to answer, Mrs. Lynden stopped him. "I'm sorry, Jerry, but I can't hear you. Why don't you take your hand away from your mouth? It'll help us understand what you're saying."

The boy next to him snickered, and everyone turned in Jerry's direction. Jerry felt like he was only one inch high. Towering heads and eyes looked down on him, waiting to see his braces. Jerry felt the warm blood come into his face and knew he was turning red. Every thought flew out of his mind. His tongue refused to move. For the rest of the hour Jerry felt miserable.

As the class ended, Mrs. Lynden reminded them about the bike trip and picnic the following Saturday. "Meet here at the church at 10 o'clock. Bring enough lunch for yourself. We'll take the old trail to the park."

Once before the class had biked together. Jerry had had a good time and looked forward to this trip. But now. . . .

When Jerry woke on Saturday, he still felt uncomfortable about his braces. As he pedaled into the church parking lot, he saw Laura laughing with the other kids. Skidding to a stop, he pulled alongside.

"Hi, Jerry!" the kids called out. Laura even remembered his name. But when Jerry said hi back, he thought of his braces and remembered not to smile. He caught Laura's quick look and turned his head away.

Getting off his bike, Jerry pretended he needed to check his tires. When he looked up, he saw Laura watching. She started to smile, but again Jerry turned away.

Soon all the kids were there and ready to leave. "I'll take the lead," said Mrs. Lynden. "Will you go last, Jerry? Just make sure everyone gets along okay."

While the kids fell into line, Jerry waited. Those who knew each other best went first. Laura pulled into line just ahead of Jerry.

Except for a few places with loose gravel, the packed dirt of the trail made the biking easy. Winding between trees, the path followed the twisting banks of a creek.

As time went on, the sun grew warm. The morning breeze died down. Now and then the bikers worked hard to conquer a hill, but going down the other side made up for it.

Spacing himself, Jerry held back so he could swoop down the hills. As he came to the top of a rise, he heard a yell. Speeding up, he saw Laura lying at the bottom in a heap, her legs and arms tangled with her bike.

Jerry soon reached her. Dirt smudged her face. She looked shaky and scared.

"Are you okay?" asked Jerry, kneeling on the ground beside her.

Laura nodded. "I mean, not really, but yeah. . . ."

Her mouth turned up, trying to smile, but she didn't make it. Instead, she looked ready to cry.

Jerry started to move her bike away. As he helped her sit up, Laura winced.

"I'm sorry!" said Jerry. "Where does it hurt?"

Then he saw the gravel ground into her skinned

knees. "Ouch," he said. "When you wipe out, you do it big."

This time the smile reached Laura's eyes.

Jerry kept talking, trying to make her feel better. In a few minutes, Laura stood up and managed to get back on her bike.

They took the rest of the trail at a slow pace. Just before they caught up to the others, Laura smiled shyly. "I thought you were an old crab apple. You never smiled."

"My braces!" thought Jerry. "I forgot all about them!" But it didn't matter anymore. He and Laura were friends.

TO TALK ABOUT

▶ How did Jerry act whenever he thought about his braces? What happened when he forgot about them?

▶ What do you suppose Laura thought about Jerry's braces?

▶ How did thinking about himself keep Jerry from making a new friend?

▶ If you feel shy about making friends, it helps to ask questions. The other person begins talking, and you forget about yourself. What are some questions to ask a kid you've just met?

Encourage one another and help one another, just as you are now doing. (1 Thessalonians 5:11, GNB)

Thank You, Jesus, that things like braces don't last forever. Help me forget the things I can't change and think about how others feel. Thanks for the new friends You're going to give me!

WEDDING IN THE FAMILY

With a final look in the mirror, Kim pushed back a strand of her blond hair. Then she lined up in front of her sisters, Becca and Anne.

As the shortest bridesmaid, she would lead the others down the aisle. The youngest of four sisters, Kim often felt like a tagalong. Too old to be a flower girl, much younger than all the others, Kim had wondered if she'd be in the wedding.

Soon after her engagement, her sister Carolyn settled the problem. "When I marry Mick, I want you with us. You're my junior bridesmaid! Okay?"

From that day on, Kim felt excited, just thinking about the big moment. But now she wished she could look as nice as her older sisters.

Nervously she touched the soft folds of her long blue dress. As she shifted her bouquet from one hand to the other, she saw that every church pew was filled. Suddenly the aisle seemed very long.

Becca leaned forward. "Hey, you look super!"

Kim turned. "Oh, don't kid me! I wish I looked as nice as you."

Becca shook her head, but before she could answer, the signal came.

Kim started down the aisle, remembering to walk slowly. Arriving at the steps, she managed to get up them without tripping on her dress. Then she turned and looked toward the back.

Next came Becca and Anne. Then Carolyn started forward. "I've never seen her so beautiful!" thought Kim.

Carolyn's face shone. When she and Mick turned toward the altar, he looked just as dreamy-eyed.

"No one will ever love me like that!" thought Kim.

During the message she wondered if everyone was looking at her. She had all she could do not to fidget. But soon Carolyn and Mick exchanged rings, and it was time for Kim to walk back up the aisle.

At the wedding reception, Grandma found her. "Kim, your hair is lovely that way!"

"Oh, Grandma, I just couldn't get it the way I wanted!"

"You couldn't possibly improve on how it is," answered Grandma. "And your dress brings out the color in your eyes."

Kim sighed. "I don't like the way it looks on me. Becca looks so much nicer than I do."

Grandma's smile faded. Her voice was gentle, yet firm. "Kimberly, I was giving you a compliment."

Grandma moved away, and Kim felt uneasy. "What does she mean?"

As she watched, Grandma walked over to Becca and her boyfriend, Steve. Looking at Becca, then at Grandma, Steve grinned. Kim heard the low rumble of his voice.

"How about this girl? I've got a pretty good one, don't you think, Grandma?"

Becca blushed, but smiled back. "Thank you! I'm glad you like the way I am."

Steve's slow smile reached his eyes. In that moment, something clicked in Kim's mind. "That's what Grandma means!"

As Becca and Steve turned toward Kim, Steve let out a low whistle. "Whew! You're all grown up! Thought that was your sister Anne walking over here!"

Out of long habit Kim almost answered, "Oh, no, I don't look as nice as Anne."

But in that instant she remembered Grandma. Kim found some words to match her grownup look. "Thanks, Steve. I'm glad you like the way I look."

When Becca and Grandma smiled, Kim knew she'd given the right answer.

TO TALK ABOUT

▶What is a compliment?

▶When Becca and Grandma complimented Kim, what did she do to herself? How do you suppose Kim's answers made Grandma and Becca feel? Why did it sound like Kim wanted more compliments?

▶If you respond to a compliment in the right way, you not only say thank you, you make the other person feel good about giving the compliment. How did Becca make Steve feel that way? What did she say?

▶Can you think of a time when someone complimented you? What did that person say? How did it make you feel? What would be a good way to answer that compliment?

▶When we turn the tables and *give* a compliment, it's important to pick out something we honestly like. Otherwise, what we say doesn't ring true and sounds phony. Is there someone you'd like to encourage by giving a compliment? What can you say?

Kind words are like honey—sweet to the taste and good for your health. (Proverbs 16:24, GNB)

Thank You, Jesus, that compliments are special gifts. Thanks for the way they make me feel. Help me know what to say when people compliment me. And help me encourage others with honest compliments.

LITTLE BROTHER

Mitch stood at the door of his bedroom. He felt like a Fourth of July firecracker with a short fuse. Another second and his temper would explode.

"It's bad enough sharing a room with Jesse," thought Mitch. "Now he's playing with my models!"

Only last night Mitch had finished a new rocket. Carefully he set it on top of the dresser, far back so no one would knock it off. But Jesse had it on the floor, playing with it.

"Jes-s-s-see!" shouted Mitch.

His little brother looked up, and tried to hide the model behind his back. Instead, his hand slipped and came down hard. The fins of the rocket broke off.

Mitch exploded. Grabbing Jesse under the arms, he picked him up and shook him.

Jesse screamed. "Put me down! Mom-m-m-m-my! Mom-m-m-m-m-my!"

Mitch set Jesse down, yet Mitch's anger didn't go away. He'd worked hard on that model. He had big dreams for how it would go into orbit.

"You can yell all you want," he told Jesse. "Mom's not here. I'm in charge, and you're gonna mind me!"

Jesse's eyes filled with tears. As soon as he got away from Mitch, he slid under the bunk bed. Mitch crouched down by the bed, knowing he'd never been so mad.

"Why do you keep doing this, Jesse?" he asked. "You know you're not supposed to touch my models."

From his hiding place under the bed, Jesse was silent.

"Why do you keep doing it?" Mitch demanded.

Still Jesse didn't answer.

Mitch reached under the bed. Grabbing Jesse's arm, he started pulling him out. But just then he caught sight of his little brother's eyes. They were filled with panic.

Mitch felt ashamed. "Sure, Jesse did something wrong," thought Mitch, dropping the little boy's arm. "He took my prize model. But. . . ."

Mitch backed off and sat down on the floor. "Okay, Jesse, come on out."

Jesse didn't move.

"Come on out, I said."

Slowly and quietly Jesse moved out, then huddled in the corner farthest from Mitch.

"What do you say, Jesse?"

Jesse drew a sobbing breath. Mitch could hardly hear his words. "I'm sorry."

Mitch groaned. "Okay, I forgive you. But it's not gonna happen again, do you hear?"

Slowly Jesse nodded, his small lips puckered, the tears spilling out of his eyes onto his cheeks.

"If you forget, I'm gonna. . . ."

Mitch stopped. "Is this the little brother I *wanted*?" he asked himself. He could remember praying for a brother. And now. . . .

Again Mitch felt ashamed. Ashamed about how mad he felt. Ashamed that he wanted to beat Jesse up. Sitting there on the floor, Mitch offered a quick, silent prayer. "Help me, God. Jesse shouldn't have taken the rocket, but what about me? What should I do?"

For a moment longer Mitch sat there. "Hmmmm. Why haven't I thought of that before?"

Then he jumped up. "Come on, Jesse, I need some help."

His little brother came out of the corner slowly. Together they went to the basement and found the old painted boards Mitch remembered seeing. "Somewhere there are some bricks," he told Jesse.

When they discovered those in the garage, Mitch carried everything to the bedroom. Before long, he put together a bookshelf.

"Okay," he said to Jesse. "From now on, this one's yours." He patted the shelf closest to the floor.

"And this one's mine." Mitch pointed to the top shelf. "I'll put my models here. You can see them, but you don't touch one thing on this shelf. Okay?"

The little boy nodded.

"Promise?" asked Mitch, still wondering if Jesse would remember.

"Promise," said Jesse, nodding his head.

"Tell you what," said Mitch. "If you don't touch my rockets, I'll take you to the field when I fly them. Not every time. But the first time they go up. Okay?"

"Promise?" asked Jesse, his eyes lighting up.

"Promise," said Mitch.

Looking at his little brother, Mitch decided he wasn't such a bad little kid after all.

TO TALK ABOUT

▶Why is it important that Jesse learns to not touch Mitch's things?

▶Why is it necessary that Mitch learns to control his temper?

▶What choices did Mitch make in working out his problem?

▶Do you think his solution is going to work? Why or why not?

▶Do you have a little brother or sister who makes you mad?

▶What are some of the problems you face? What are some ways you can solve those problems?

It is better to be slow-tempered than famous; it is better to have self-control than to control an army. (Proverbs 16:32, TLB)

Forgive me, Jesus, when I let my temper get out of control. Help me talk and pray about the things that make me mad. Help me work out ways to change them.

SHAWNA MAKES
A HIGHDIVE

Step by step, Shawna climbed the ladder to the highdive. Reaching the board, she looked down. At one side of the pool Alex and Lucy lay sunning themselves.

They had all come to the pool together, and Shawna liked them. They always seemed more exciting than the kids she knew at church. But Shawna never felt sure how Alex and Lucy felt about her. She always wondered, "Do they really like me? I don't feel like I fit in."

Then Shawna thought about her dive. She never grew tired of those seconds between the board and the water. Most of the time she felt excited, but also scared.

"When you get started, keep going," Mom told her once. "Don't change your mind in the middle of the air."

Whenever Mom and Dad could, they cheered Shawna on. Just thinking about them helped her sometimes.

Now Shawna took three quick steps and a jump, and landed on the end of the board. Springing into the air, she spread her arms wide in a swan dive. Her body made the arc, swung down. An instant later she brought her arms above her head and sliced the water like a knife.

As Shawna rose to the surface, she felt excited. "That was a good one!" she thought. Wiping the water out of her eyes, she looked around. Alex and Lucy were sitting up. "They're so busy talking, did they see my dive?"

Shawna's strokes slowed, then stopped, as she reached the edge of the pool. Pulling herself from the water, she tried to shrug aside her left-out feeling. As she lay down on her towel, she looked like one of them. But inside she felt set apart from Lucy and Alex. She wanted to belong.

Alex looked her way. "Ready to go?"

"We've only been here half an hour," Shawna answered, surprise in her voice. "What's the big rush?"

But Alex's dark eyes looked bored. He was ready to

move on, and Shawna knew Lucy would go with him. She'd do whatever Alex did.

"Is this another highdive?" wondered Shawna. "I want to go with them, but. . . ."

Picking up her towel and sunglasses, she stood up, trying to push aside her uneasiness. As they left the pool, Alex led the way. Soon he swung onto a path leading to the trees on the far side of the park. His lazy smile creased his face. "Good dive you made."

Shawna warmed to his praise. "Oh, thanks!" But a moment later her uneasiness returned. "Where're we going?" she asked.

Without answering, Alex kept moving, with Lucy at his side. Suddenly Shawna guessed why they headed for the trees. Was it their new meeting place? Her steps slowed.

Alex turned. "Come on. What's taking so long?"

Looking at him, Shawna thought again how much she liked him, how much she'd like to fit in with his friends. Yet she felt a mysterious hand pushing her toward something that made her afraid.

"What will it be this time?" she wondered. "Booze? Pot? Drugs?"

As they neared the trees, Shawna smelled the scent of pot. "I don't wanna smoke a joint," she said, stopping on the path.

"It won't hurt you any."

"That's not true," Shawna told him. "It's the worst

thing you can do to your lungs, and it's not good for your brain, either."

Alex smirked. "Are you nuts?"

Shawna hated Alex's laugh. It had a hard sound to it and always made her feel left out. "Maybe I should give it a try," she thought. "Maybe I'd fit in."

"Everybody does it," said Alex. Lucy looked like she agreed.

"I know it's bad for me," thought Shawna with one part of her mind. The other part tried to push that thought aside. "Nothing would ever happen to *me*."

Then she remembered what Mom had said. "Don't change your mind in the middle of the air."

Shawna drew a deep breath. "I don't wanna smoke a joint," she said again. "I'm going back to the pool."

"What are you, chicken or something? Or do you think you're better than us?"

Knifelike, the words cut. Shawna looked Alex in the eye. "I said no, and I mean no. Don't ever ask me again."

Turning, she started back to the pool—half running, half walking so Alex wouldn't see the tears in her eyes.

Then she heard a voice behind her. "Hey, just a minute," called Lucy. "I'm coming with you."

As Lucy caught up, Shawna slowed her steps and blinked away the tears.

TO TALK ABOUT

▶Why do kids who are Christians still face temptations? Do you think Shawna stuck to her decision to say no? Why or why not?

▶What was Alex offering Shawna—friendship or the pressure to do something that would hurt her? How do you know?

▶Do you feel Alex was a true friend? Does a true friend hurt a friend on purpose?

▶Is it worth having a friend like Alex? Why or why not?

▶If you want to be popular, how can it affect the choices you make?

▶Shawna wanted to fit in with Alex and his friends, yet she felt uneasy. A feeling of uneasiness can be the Holy Spirit's warning. Why is it *good* if you feel uncomfortable with some kids? How can that feeling protect you?

▶What does it mean to stand firm in a choice? How can you say no so kids know you really mean it?

▶What if you don't have a dad or mom who supports you in making right choices? Where could you find supportive friends and adults?

▶What are some Bible verses that can help you in hard times? How can it help you to memorize those verses?

The LORD said, "When you pass through the waters, I will be with you; and when you pass through the rivers, they will not sweep over you." (Isaiah 43:2)

Thank You, Jesus, that I don't feel comfortable with some kids. Thanks for protecting me that way. Whenever I face something that would hurt me, give me the strength to say no and stick to it.

MICHAEL'S TREEHOUSE

For Michael the July afternoon seemed to last forever. "If I still lived in Annandale, I'd have plenty to do," he thought. But two weeks before, he and Mom and Dad had moved here. So far Michael hadn't made any friends.

Before moving, he knew lots of kids, and most of them he liked. It didn't seem to matter that he had no brothers or sisters. Now the house seemed awfully quiet when he was home alone. Often he'd turn up the volume on his boombox, trying to fill the empty spaces. Today not even music helped.

Then he made a discovery. As soon as Dad drove into the garage, Michael pounced on him. "Do you see this stuff the other people left? Can I have the two-byfours, and those old storm windows, and the boards leaning against the wall?"

Dad held up his hands. "Hey, slow down! Why do you need them?"

"I've always wanted a treehouse. We've never had a place for one before."

"Hmmm," said Dad, not seeming surprised. Michael was always thinking up projects. "Where do you want it?"

Michael led the way to the back yard and pointed out a huge oak. "See those two branches?" Walking around the trunk, he pointed upward. "The door could be right there, and the ladder on this side."

"Hmmm," said Dad again.

"Three windows—one on each side, except where the door is."

"Wellll," Dad walked around the tree, checking it from every angle. "Yep. It would work. But I'd like to help a bit so we can make it safe."

"All riiiight!" exclaimed Michael.

And so, the work began. Dad and Michael went to the lumberyard and bought extra-long two-by-sixes. That night they nailed one of them across two branches and over to the trunk. They used the other as an extra brace, stretching to a nearby maple.

Early the next morning Michael and his dad started again. Soon they had a base for the floor. Then the walls went up.

At last the treehouse was finished. Dad climbed down the ladder. "Well, Michael, it's all yours!"

"Hey, that's right," said Michael, feeling proud of what they'd built. "It's all mine!"

Just then a boy rode his bike through the alley. Seeing the treehouse, he skidded to a stop. "I'm Sam," he said to Michael. "I live a couple blocks from here."

As soon as Michael introduced himself, Sam exclaimed, "What a great treehouse! Can I see it, Mike?"

"Uh, sure," said Michael, thinking it seemed strange to be called Mike again. Only his friends in Annandale called him that. Rung by rung he led the way.

Sam followed him. "Wow!" he said, looking out the windows. "What a great clubhouse this would be!"

For a moment a secret hope filled Michael. "A club?" Joining Sam at a window, he looked down through the leaves. "What do you mean?"

"Jim and Randy and I have a club. We've been looking for a place to meet."

"Would I have some friends?" Michael wondered. "Maybe it'd be really fun!" But he was afraid to let himself hope.

Then he had an awful thought. "What if they wrecked the house?" In Annandale he'd let a kid borrow his bike. When the kid totaled it, he never paid Michael back.

Feeling torn inside, Michael wondered what to say. He was still wondering when he started back down the ladder. "I want new friends," he thought. "But I'm scared. What should I do?"

As Michael reached the ground, he figured it out. "I'll show 'em how to take care of it," he thought. "We'll have some club rules."

As Sam swung onto his bike, he grinned. "So long, Mike. I'll bring back the guys. Okay?"

"Okay!" said Mike. And inside he felt okay, too.

TO TALK ABOUT

▶If Mike chooses to share the treehouse, what do you think will happen to his loneliness? How can sharing be a way of making friends?

▶When you share, it doesn't mean you let kids do whatever they want with your things. They should respect your rights. Do you think Mike's new friends will be careful with the treehouse? What can he do if they aren't?

▶What did you discover during a time when you were afraid to share and it worked out all right?

▶Like Michael, all of us need friends. We also need to know that God can help us if we're lonely. How has God helped you when you've been lonely?

Jesus said, "Give to others, and God will give to
you. . . . The measure you use for others is the one
that God will use for you." (Luke 6:38, GNB)

When I'm lonely, Lord, remind me that You're with
me. Show me how to share and how to make new
friends. Thanks for being my best Friend.

FRIENDS AT ANY PRICE?

For as long as Sondra could remember, Erin had been her best friend at church. Sondra liked it that way. It made her feel good to know that when the kids got together, she had someone special to do things with.

But now it looked like that might change.

When the kids met at church to go bowling, a new girl showed up. For a few minutes she hung around the door, as though wondering if she should duck out.

As Sondra watched, Erin went over to her. "I don't know your name," Sondra heard her say. "Are you new here?"

The girl nodded. "I'm Jody Langseth. We just moved here from Cleveland."

Soon Erin brought her over. "Jody, this is my friend Sondra."

Sondra smiled at Jody, but her heart wasn't in it. She didn't try to make her feel at home.

Erin didn't seem to notice. "My dad's driving us to the bowling alley," she told Jody. "You can ride with Sondra and me."

When they reached the alley, the girls discovered the boys had taken over most of the lanes. Sondra had expected to bowl with Erin. But there were only two places left on one lane and two on another.

As they waited in line for balls and shoes, Erin whispered to Sondra. "I'll bowl with Jody since she doesn't know anyone. Why don't you and Mary get together?"

Feeling lost and alone, Sondra found Mary. She didn't want to bowl with her. She didn't like the boys on their lane. She just wanted to keep Erin to herself. She wanted everything to be the way it used to be.

Two lanes over, Erin and Jody started bowling. Watching them, Sondra felt uneasy. "What if Erin likes Jody so much that she doesn't like *me* anymore?"

Trying to push the thought aside, Sondra picked up her ball. Her first try knocked down two pins. Her next ball rolled into the gutter.

Sondra pasted on a smile and hoped for better on her next turn. But her entire game was off. Whenever she sat down, she tried to watch two lanes over. She kept telling herself, "I wish I was there."

When they started the next game, Mary tried to cheer up Sondra. "Hey, come on, you can do better. You're a good bowler."

But just then Sondra heard a shout. Jody had gotten a strike! Watching Erin slap Jody on the back, Sondra felt left out again.

In the second game she bowled even worse. A new thought haunted her. "What if I lose my best friend?"

Going back to the church, the girls were separated again. But Sondra slipped into the food line behind Erin. "How did you bowl?" she asked.

"Great!" answered Erin.

Jody turned around to listen, and Sondra ignored her. "Did you do better than the boys you were with?" she asked, still looking at Erin.

"Nope," said Erin. "But that's okay. It was Jody's first time bowling, and guess what? She got a strike!"

Still Sondra didn't look at Jody. Nor did she say, "Congrats!" When she picked up her hamburger, Sondra saw the strange look in Jody's eyes. Half question, half hurt. Her look seemed to ask, "Is there something wrong with me?"

As she sat down at a table, Sondra saw Erin's face. "Uh-oh," she thought.

Suddenly a feeling of shame started way down in Sondra's toes. In that moment she didn't like herself. She didn't like the way she'd treated Jody.

But there was something that bothered her even more. "Erin knows I'm cutting Jody out," Sondra thought. "She doesn't like it."

Sitting there between Erin and Jody, Sondra asked herself one question: "What should I do?"

TO TALK ABOUT

▶In what ways did Sondra want to keep Erin for herself?

▶Why is it easy to cut out someone who's new? How did Sondra do it to Jody?

▶The Bible tells us that "love is not self-seeking." What does it mean to be self-seeking? How was Sondra self-seeking? Why do you think this story is called "Friends at Any Price"?

▶Has anyone ever treated you the way Sondra treated Jody? How did it feel to be ignored for a reason you didn't understand?

▶Why did Sondra treat Jody that way? What was she feeling inside? Have you ever felt that way when you thought you'd lose a good friend? What happened?

▶To have a good relationship it's important to give a friend enough space. What does it mean to give someone space? Why do good friends need to give each other enough space to also be friends with other kids?

▶What is the best way to keep a good friend?

[Love] is not rude, it is not self-seeking, it is not easily angered, it keeps no record of wrongs.
(1 Corinthians 13:5)

Help me, Jesus, when I get selfish and want to keep a friend all to myself. Help me give my friends the space they need to keep on being my friends.

her neck and in back of her ears.

Now Paula broke into Debbie's thoughts. "Just because you won a blue ribbon last year doesn't mean you'll do it again."

"Is that what's bugging you? Because you got a red ribbon?"

"Don't be dumb," answered Paula. "The judge was playing favorites."

Once more Debbie's anger boiled up. As she brushed Oreo until her coat shone, she couldn't get Paula out of her mind. Debbie didn't like being enemies with someone. Usually she found it easy to make friends. She'd even done it with a calf.

Just then an idea dropped into her mind. "Aha!" she thought, bending down to hide her grin from Paula. "I'll be as nice to her as I am to Oreo."

While clipping the hair around Oreo's ears, Debbie decided what to do. She felt like she'd be spitting through her teeth, but she'd give it a try.

When Paula finished brushing Princess, Debbie turned to her. "Her coat looks nice and shiny."

Paula looked surprised, but didn't say anything.

"You've done a good job of grooming her."

Still Paula looked surprised, as though she didn't quite trust Debbie. But this time she mumbled a thanks.

As Debbie twisted the end of Oreo's tail into many small braids, she felt different inside. She still didn't like being next to Paula, but at least she didn't feel as mad.

The next day Debbie unbraided Oreo's tail and backcombed the kinky ends. As she fluffed them up, Debbie looked over at Paula. "Your heifer looks great."

Again Paula looked like she didn't know if Debbie was teasing her. After a moment Paula seemed to decide Debbie meant it. "So does yours," she said, her voice low.

When it was time for the judging, Debbie changed into white clothes. If there was a tie, even the appearance of the one showing the animal could make a difference in winning or losing. Then she attached a lead to Oreo's halter and fell into line. Paula and Princess followed them into the large open space surrounded by bleachers.

As they walked in a circle, the judge called out, "Stop your heifers!" Then, "Pose them!"

Oreo stood with her front legs firmly beneath her. With the back leg closest to the judge forward, she kept the other leg straight.

Soon the judge began pulling animals out of the circle and placing them in lines—one line for the blue ribbons, another for the red, and so on. When the judge placed Oreo at the front of the first line, Debbie felt excited. "Maybe she'll get Grand Champion of our class!" she thought.

Paula's turn was next. The judge circled Princess,

and Paula kept moving to the opposite side so she wouldn't block the judge's view. She looked sure of herself and Princess.

Debbie caught her breath. For the first time she wondered, "Was Paula bugging me so I'd feel jumpy and not do as well?"

A moment later the judge led Paula forward, putting her in front of Debbie.

Outwardly Debbie stood at attention, but on the inside, she felt sick. "Paula's first, and I'm second. She'll get Grand Champion."

Then Debbie had an even worse thought, "Did I help Paula win by being nice to her? She looks so sure of herself." In close competition Paula's attitude could make a difference.

As the judge circled the other calves, the awful question stayed with Debbie. Watching the judge, Debbie kept Oreo alert. But she saw Paula glance toward the stands and smile.

In that moment the judge looked their way. "He must have seen Paula," thought Debbie. "She shouldn't have looked at the stands. She looks *too* sure of herself."

The judge returned to their line, and asked Debbie more questions. When he told her to move in front of Paula, Debbie hardly dared breathe.

A moment later the judge brought out the Grand Champion ribbon. "I place Oreo at the top of the class," he called out. "She's an outstanding heifer, and responds well to her owner."

Then the judge handed the ribbon and trophy to Debbie.

Grand Champion? Best in show? Debbie felt like

crying and laughing at the same time.

The judge moved on, and gave Paula a blue ribbon. Watching her, Debbie wondered, "How's she gonna feel—missing it by one dumb move?"

Soon they began leading their heifers back to the shed. Debbie felt like shouting. Paula was quiet the whole way.

But when they finally stopped and tied their calves to the rail, she looked at Debbie. "Congrats,"

Paula said. "You really deserved it."

"Thanks!" said Debbie. Then she flung her arms around Oreo. "I've won more than a trophy," she thought.

TO TALK ABOUT

▶What did Debbie mean by thinking, "I've won more than a trophy"?

▶Why is it especially hard to be nice to someone you compete against?

▶Debbie learned something from Oreo that helped her decide how to act toward Paula. What was it?

▶How does cutting down another person destroy a friendship? Why does encouragement help a friendship?

▶Do you have a pet you love very much? If so, why does that animal mean a lot to you?

▶How has your pet helped you know how to act with people?

When you please the LORD, you can make your enemies into friends. (Proverbs 16:7, GNB)

*Thank You, God, for creating animals. Thanks for
how much my pet means to me. When kids bug me,
help me act in a way that pleases You. Thanks that
You can turn even my enemies into friends.*

SOMEONE IN THE KITCHEN

"See you, Joey!"

Brian waved goodbye and started up the driveway. He was whistling when he reached the house. It had been a good day at school.

But when he came to the door, he stopped. As though putting on a mask, he let his face go blank. Not for anything would he let his stepmother know that things had gone better.

The night before, Marcy and Dad had prayed for him. "I won't tell her about it," Brian decided. "She'll think it's because they prayed."

For the millionth time Brian thought about Mom. She had died two years ago, but sometimes he still ached inside. "It was bad enough for her to die. Why

83

did Dad have to get married again?"

Marcy was in the kitchen when Brian walked in. "How'd it go today?" she asked.

Usually Brian pretended he didn't hear her, but this time he couldn't. "Oh, I don't know," he said, and kept moving.

As he came to the family room, he stopped in his tracks. "You changed it!"

"I worked on it all day," said Marcy. "How do you like it?"

"I don't." Brian kicked at the sofa. "I can't stand it. Why did you change it?"

Marcy blinked. Something deep in her eyes looked hurt. Then the moment passed.

Marcy sighed. "It's important that the house feels comfortable to me—that it reflects my tastes. . . ."

Brian broke in. "I don't like your tastes. I like the way Mom left it."

Again Brian saw the shadow deep in Marcy's eyes. She walked over to a window. For a moment she stood there, looking out. When she turned back, the hurt look was gone.

"I'm not trying to take your mother's place, Brian. She was a lovely woman. But none of us can change the fact that she died."

This time Brian turned away. He didn't want to listen, but Marcy kept on.

"Your dad and I were both lonely. We love each

other. And he felt he needed my help. . . ."

Marcy's voice sounded strange. In spite of himself, Brian looked at her.

"I'm not perfect," she said. "But I'm trying my best. You can choose to like me or not like me. If you decide you don't want to like me, there's nothing I can do about it."

Brian squirmed. "Old witch!" he thought. He knew what Marcy was saying was right, but he didn't want to think about it. It made him too uncomfortable. Yet he had to admit Marcy had guts.

As soon as he could, Brian escaped to his room. When he came to supper, he picked at his meal. If Marcy tried to talk with him, he looked at his plate and mumbled. But when Dad spoke, Brian acted interested and answered his questions.

In the days that followed, Brian often felt torn apart inside. Sometimes he felt lonesome for Mom. If only she could come back, they'd have good talks again.

Mom had been sick for a long time. Sometimes Brian wondered if it was his fault that she died. Whenever he thought about that, he took it out on Marcy. He picked apart everything she did, even the cookies she baked.

"Why didn't you make chocolate chip instead of peanut butter?" he asked her one day. "I don't like peanut butter." Yet when she wasn't around, he sneaked the cookies out of the kitchen.

Sometimes he heard Dad and Marcy laugh together. Brian knew that when he was with them, they never did. "Good," he thought. "I'm making her feel bad."

Then one day everything changed. When Brian came home from school, Marcy wasn't there. The house was empty. A note on the table told him she needed to fly home.

At supper Dad said, "Her mother's very sick. Marcy's the only one who can help."

It wasn't long before Brian got tired of eating TV dinners again. He'd forgotten what it was like to wash his own clothes. But most of all, he missed having someone in the kitchen when he came home. He missed *her*.

Finally one day Brian asked, "When's Marcy coming back?"

"I don't know," answered Dad. "She's trying to find an opening for her mother in a nursing home. Her mom's too sick to fly here."

As the weeks stretched into a month, Brian noticed the empty house even more. One afternoon he thought about how he felt whenever he was mean to Marcy. "When I try to hate her, I find all kinds of things wrong with her."

A strange new thought came to him. "You can choose to like me," Marcy had said.

That night Brian made a choice. Long ago Mom had told him how to pray. And so, he asked, "Jesus, please forgive me. Forgive me for all the mean things I've said to Marcy."

A few days passed, and Brian's struggle faded into the background. But one day the next week, Marcy was in the kitchen when Brian came home. When he saw her, he remembered his prayer. Suddenly he felt scared. "Oh, wow! What do I do now?"

TO TALK ABOUT

▶After someone dies, people often feel guilty about something that couldn't be helped. How do you know it wasn't Brian's fault that his mother died?

▶How did his guilty feelings hurt his relationship with Marcy?

▶If you choose to *not* like someone, what kind of things do you notice about that person?

▶If you choose to like someone, what kind of things do you notice?

▶Is there someone you often have to be with, even though you don't like that person? What happens?

▶What choice can you make? How do you think it will affect the way you feel about each other?

87

We love because God first loved us. (1 John 4:19, GNB)

When I feel mixed up inside, I take it out on people around me. Forgive me, Jesus. Help me sort out my feelings. I choose to like the people I need to get along with. Help me see good things about them.

88

BECKY'S
CHOICE

"Beck-e-e-e-e!" came a little voice from the bedroom.

"Just a minute," said Becky into the phone. She was babysitting at the O'Connors again. Cupping her hand over the receiver, she called out, "I'll be there soon, Kristin."

"You said that last time," answered the little voice.

For a moment everything was quiet. Becky cradled the phone on her shoulder and slid into a more comfortable position. Soon she forgot about Kristin.

A loud crash broke into her conversation. Becky jumped up, filled with panic. "What happened?" she wondered, running for Kristin's bedroom. No one there.

89

"Where are you, Kristin?" Becky called out. "Kri-i-i-i-stin!"

Becky heard a little sound. Heading down the hall, she came to the O'Connors' bedroom. As she tried to open the door, it stopped partway.

Looking down, Becky discovered the reason. A large piece from a glass lamp had spun across the hardwood floor. Other pieces lay all around one side of the bed. And on the bed sat Kristin, looking scared.

"Kristin, shame on you!" snapped Becky. "You're supposed to be in bed. What are you doing in here?"

Tears welled up in Kristin's eyes. "You didn't come when I called you." The tears started to slide down her cheeks. "I want my mommy."

Becky looked at Kristin, then looked at the floor. "I'm in big trouble," she thought. "What am I gonna tell her mom and dad?"

Then another thought struck her. "Kristin must have pushed the lamp off the bedside table. What if she'd been on the floor and *pulled* it off?" It wasn't hard to imagine a little girl all cut up with flying glass.

Becky didn't want to face the truth, yet it pounded away at her. "It was really my fault, wasn't it, God?"

In that moment Becky didn't like herself very much.

Just then she remembered the phone. Going around to the side clear of glass, Becky crawled onto the bed, and picked up Kristin. Carrying her to the living room, she spoke into the phone. "Gotta go. Can't talk now."

Sitting down in a big rocker, Becky tried to comfort Kristin. But the little girl's sobs increased.

Just then the phone jangled. "We've been trying to reach you for over an hour," said Mrs. O'Connor. "We couldn't get through because of the busy signal. Is everything okay?"

For a moment Becky wanted to lie, and pretend nothing had happened. She wanted to act as if it was all Kristin's fault. But as she opened her mouth to make excuses, something made her stop.

Becky drew a deep breath. "We've had a problem here," she said. "But I'm taking care of it. I'll tell you about it when you get home."

"You're sure?" said Mrs. O'Connor.

"I'm sure," said Becky. "We're doing fine now."

As she hung up the phone, she made a choice—a promise to herself and to God. "I'm going to be different."

TO TALK ABOUT

▶ It would have been easy for Becky to make up excuses or lie about what happened. Why is it important for Becky's own sake that she didn't?

▶ What do you think Becky should tell the O'Connors when they come home?

▶Becky wants to become someone others can count on. What habits will she need to break in order to keep her promise to herself and to God?

▶Do you babysit, either at home, or in someone else's house? What are some ideas you could give Becky to help her become a better babysitter?

▶Sometimes babysitting seems like a boring job that can be done any way you want. Yet your relationships with the kids you babysit can be some of the most important relationships you have. Whether you're a boy or a girl, how can babysitting experience help you as you grow older?

"You have been faithful with a few things; I will put you in charge of many things." (Matthew 25:21)

Lord, I want to be faithful to You. I want to be someone other people can count on. When I babysit, help me keep the children safe. Help me love them the way You do.

92

BACK YARD DISCOVERY

"**W**ant some cookies?" asked Tim, digging deep into the jar.

Manuel was Tim's best friend and had come home with him from school. As they downed cookies and milk, they tried to decide what to do.

Just then Pete, Tim's older brother, joined them at the kitchen table. "How about shooting baskets?" he asked.

"Naw," said Tim. "Let's not." He knew what that would be like. Pete was four years older and already a top basketball player.

But Manuel was interested. When Pete said, "I'll give you some tips," it was decided.

Slowly Tim stood up and followed them out to the

hoop in front of the garage. "Why does Pete always do this?" he wondered. "Manuel's my friend, but Pete takes over."

"I'll start by shooting a basket from here," said Pete, standing directly in front of the hoop. "You try next, Manuel. If you make a basket from the same position, you get the point. If not, I get the point."

Pete's shot swished through the net. Manuel stood in the same place and his ball also dropped through.

"Good, the point's yours," said Pete. "Now, stand wherever you want. If you put it in, Tim tries from the same spot."

Manuel moved over to one side and ran in for a layup. Sure enough, he made the basket. But when Tim tried the same shot, the ball hit the hoop and bounced off.

Soon they'd each had several turns. With every shot Tim tried harder. Yet his score stayed at zero while Pete's jumped ahead.

"I can't keep up," thought Tim. "I can't even keep up with Manuel." As the gap between their scores and his widened, he felt embarrassed. Then he started feeling like a failure.

"I can't do *anything* as well as Pete," thought Tim. The more hopeless he felt, the more Pete and Manuel seemed to enjoy the game.

"Here, do it this way," Pete would say to Manuel.

"You'll get a better shot." But usually Pete forgot to help Tim. Or if he tried, Tim couldn't do what he said.

"Hey, let's do something else," said Tim to Manuel.

But Manuel wanted to keep on. Finally Tim gave up and dropped down on the nearby grass. Pete and Manuel didn't seem to notice.

"Can't stand that Pete," thought Tim. "I'll never be as good. I'm not even gonna try."

For awhile Tim sat there, watching Pete and Manuel shoot baskets. After a time, Tim noticed something had changed in the way Manuel played. He was dropping in more shots.

"Maybe Pete really helped him," thought Tim. "And Manuel cares more about basketball than I do."

Just then Manuel's long shot swished through the net. "Good one!" called Tim, forgetting about himself.

Manuel looked over and grinned. Pete motioned to Tim, for the first time noticing he'd dropped out.

"Come here," said Pete. "I'll show you how, too."

Slowly Tim stood up. "I'll never be as good," he thought. "But I don't have to wreck Manuel's fun. Guess I'd better make the best of it."

Ten minutes later Tim discovered something. When he stopped trying so hard, he started having fun.

But his biggest surprise came when he tried a new play. Pete slapped him on the back and said enthusiastically, "Hey, that's really great!"

Tim felt great on the inside, too.

TO TALK ABOUT

▶Whenever Tim was around Pete, he asked himself, "How am I doing *compared to* Pete?" Why did that question make Tim feel he was failing?

▶How did family position affect what Tim thought he could do?

▶Why do you think Tim did better when he stopped trying so hard?

▶Tim needs to make some choices. He can:

    1) wait until Manuel goes home and tell his brother to leave his friend alone;

    2) learn from Pete and try to be as good a basketball player; or

    3) try to become good in a different area—one where he doesn't have to compete with Pete.

What do you think Tim should do? Why?

▶If Tim chooses to work at basketball, why might he become a better player than other kids his age?

▶What happened when Tim forgot about himself and encouraged Manuel?

▶Sometimes kids are not good in sports but do other things well. If you feel you can't succeed in sports, what other activities can you do instead?

I was pushed back and about to fall, but the LORD helped me. (Psalm 118:13)

Show me, Jesus, when I should try to get better at something, and when I should grow in another way. Help me find something I can do well. But also help me to encourage other kids in what they can do.

SECRET BETWEEN FRIENDS

J eanie and Kate were staying overnight together. All evening they talked and giggled. Now it was late. As they stretched out on their sleeping bags, Jeanie had a question.

"Kate, do you tell me all your secrets?"

"Sure," said Kate. "Don't you tell me all yours?"

Jeanie thought about it a minute. "Wellll. . . ."

"Well, you should," said Kate. "After all, we're best friends."

Jeanie was quiet, not sure she wanted to tell Kate everything she thought and felt.

But Kate kept on. "When I tell you a secret, I know you won't tell anyone. And I wouldn't tell *anyone* your secret."

"You're sure?" asked Jeanie.

"For *sure*," answered Kate. "I wouldn't give away a secret for *anything*. Especially a secret that's yours."

Jeanie still felt uneasy. What if Kate didn't understand?

Kate rolled over on her stomach. "I've told you all my secrets. What haven't you told me?"

Jeanie's secret was so special she didn't want to tell anyone. Talking about it might spoil the special way she felt.

"Come on, Jeanie. That's what friends are for!"

"Can I really count on you?" Jeanie wondered.

"I promise not to tell a soul," said Kate, as though reading Jeanie's thoughts.

"Promise?" asked Jeanie.

"Promise," answered Kate, her brown eyes serious.

So Jeanie told Kate about Nathan, and how much she liked him. She told Kate how special Nathan acted whenever she saw him at school. And how cute he was when he smiled. And how maybe—just maybe—he liked her.

"You won't tell anyone? You promise?" asked Jeanie.

"I said promise, didn't I?" said Kate. "Your secret's safe with me."

Soon after, they fell asleep. The next morning Jeanie wondered if she'd done the right thing in telling Kate her secret. "But I can trust her," she thought.

"After all, we're best friends."

Two days later Jeanie started to worry. As she walked down the hall at school, she saw three girls in a huddle, talking and giggling.

Seeing Jeanie, they stopped talking. Like a thin sliver of light coming through a window, Jeanie felt a warning.

Later that day she knew for sure. As she ran outside for gym, the other girls started teasing her.

"Jeanie likes Nathan! Jeanie likes Nathan!" In a singsong chant the words rose all around her.

Jeanie's face grew hot with embarrassment. She tried to pretend she didn't hear. But the girls kept chanting, their voices growing louder all the time.

"What if Nathan hears them?" Jeanie thought, glancing around to see where the boys were. Sure enough, Nathan was far down the field, playing soccer. As Jeanie watched, his team took a timeout.

"Shhhhhh!" Jeanie begged. "He'll hear you. Be quiet!"

But the girls chanted louder, and Nathan's head turned in their direction.

Jeanie wished she was a turtle and could crawl inside a shell. "I'll never be able to look him in the face again," she moaned.

As soon as school was over, Jeanie hunted up Kate. "You said you were my best friend!"

"I am!" answered Kate.

"And you spread it all over school that I like Nathan. I've never been more embarrassed in my life!"

"What? All over school? No, I didn't!"

"Yes, you did!"

"Says who?"

"Says me. How else could the whole school know?"

"You're kidding!" said Kate. "Really?"

"Really."

"I only told one person. Shelley promised. . . ."

"That she'd never say a word. . . ."

"Oh, Jeanie! I'm so sorry! I really, really am. Will you forgive me?"

But Jeanie wasn't ready to forgive. "Kate, you promised. And now you just say two little words—I'm sorry. I'm left with all the mess. Forever and ever!"

Kate's brown eyes filled with tears. "Jeanie, I really am sorry. I'm sorry I told. I'm sorry I hurt you."

Jeanie glared at her. "What should I say?" she wondered. "Can I ever count on her again?"

TO TALK ABOUT

▶Why is it hard to keep a secret? Why do you feel more important if you have a secret to tell?

▶Why was it especially harmful that Kate told this secret of Jeanie's?

▶What does it mean to trust someone? How did Jeanie trust Kate?

▶How did Kate destroy Jeanie's trust in her?

▶Do you think Jeanie should forgive Kate? Why or why not?

▶In what way could Jeanie show her love to Kate by giving her a second chance? Do you think she should do that? Why do you feel that way?

▶Do you think Jeanie should ever tell Kate another secret? Why or why not?

▶When is it important to tell a parent or other adult a secret between kids? Why might talking at that time keep someone from getting hurt?

If you want people to like you, forgive them when they wrong you. Remembering wrongs can break up a friendship. (Proverbs 17:9, GNB)

Jesus, help me both ways. When I need to ask for-giveness, give me the courage to do it. When I need to forgive someone, help me remember how often You've forgiven me. Help me be someone others can trust.

FAMILY CHRISTMAS

"Can we cut our own Christmas tree this year?" asked Darren.

"Good idea," answered Dad, pushing aside his dinner plate. "When do you want to do it?"

"How about tomorrow afternoon? It's Saturday."

"Wellllll," Darren felt sure Dad didn't want to say it, but there'd be football on TV. Dad really liked to watch.

Darren's older sister, Cheryl, jumped in. "I want to go Christmas shopping with LuAnn tomorrow."

"I really need to bake Christmas cookies," said Mom.

"And I wanna go ice skating with Jay," said Darren's little brother, Scottie.

"Hey, we never do stuff together anymore!" Darren exclaimed.

"Darren's right," said Dad. "How about it? I think we should go."

"Oh, Daaadd!" complained Cheryl.

"No, I mean it," said Dad. "Darren's right. Every one of us is going to have to give up something, but. . . ."

Mom looked at him and smiled. "How about everyone just eating fewer cookies?"

Dad grinned, and Darren hoped Mom didn't really mean it. That would be awful.

Scottie was the hardest to convince, but finally he said yes. The next afternoon everyone piled into the station wagon. Even their collie, Ruff, went along.

When they reached the Christmas tree farm, Darren snapped on Ruff's leash. Dad took a saw out of the back of the car. The man who owned the trees told them where to go, then left them on their own.

Once away from the buildings, Darren let Ruff go. Instantly the collie shot after a rabbit. Watching Ruff bound through the snow, Darren felt the same way inside—let loose or something.

"Hmmmm," said Dad. "It feels good to be out in the woods with all of you."

Mom smiled and took Dad's hand. Scottie trudged along behind, still mad he hadn't been able to go skating. But Cheryl was even willing to talk to Darren.

107

When they reached the Christmas trees, the family found themselves alone. The young trees filled an open field on the edge of an older woods. As Darren watched, Ruff took off again. Soon he disappeared behind the huge trunk of a fallen tree.

"Okay, spread out!" said Dad. "Find the one you like."

Each member of the family decided on a different tree. Scottie discovered a scrawny little one about his size. Mom wanted a fat tree. "It'd be perfect near the living room window."

Dad thought they should go as tall as possible and set it in the corner this year. And Cheryl wanted something altogether different—a spruce instead of a pine.

Dad grinned. "Well, Darren, you haven't picked out your favorite. Who's going to get first choice?"

"Let's have a snowball fight," said Darren. "The one who wins can pick."

"Wellll," Dad looked around. "Okay, over there, where we won't hurt the Christmas trees."

Mom laughed. "But no iceballs. And you can't hit anyone in the head."

Darren claimed the huge tree trunk on the edge of the woods. By the time Dad signaled the beginning of the fight, Darren had a stockpile of snowballs.

Mom was the first one out, but she went laughing just the same. Scottie was next. Ruff ran back and forth between snowballs.

Cheryl and Dad wanted to join forces, but Darren wouldn't let them. It took awhile, but finally he volleyed one snowball after another in their direction. Three hit Cheryl almost at one time. Dad started laughing, and Darren got him too.

"We surrender, we surrender!" Dad called out.

"Okay, Darren, it's your choice," said Mom.

Darren took a long time to make up his mind. It seemed he walked around every Christmas tree in the whole field. Finally he pointed out his choice.

"How come you want that one?" asked Mom.

"Wellll," Darren wasn't sure he should explain. Then he grinned. "It's a spruce for Cheryl, and you see here? The back side is scrawny for Scottie. It's tall for Dad and fat for Mom."

By now everyone was laughing, and Ruff barked along with them.

"And you, Darren? What do you want in a tree?" asked Dad.

Darren grinned again, and didn't answer. If he had to tell them, he wasn't sure what he'd say.

But one thing he did know—Christmas was off to a good start.

TO TALK ABOUT

▶Why is it hard for families to do something together?

109

▶What did each person have to give up in order to go for the Christmas tree?

▶What is the difference between *finding* time and *making* time for something?

▶What special things does your family like to do together? What kinds of things do you do during different seasons of the year?

▶How do those times help the members of your family laugh with each other?

▶If your mom and dad aren't living together, what do you like to do when you're with your mom? When you're with your dad?

"The joy that the LORD gives you will make you strong." (Nehemiah 8:10, GNB)

Thank You, Lord, for special family times. Thanks for times when we laugh and do things together. Make us strong as a family.

TAG-ALONG TRUDY

As Diane brushed her hair, she caught a movement in the mirror. Her little sister stood just back of her. Wobbling forward on tiptoes, Trudy tried to see herself. Turning this way and that, she managed to brush her hair just the way Diane did hers.

Diane groaned. "Will it never end?" she thought. "Whatever I do, she wants to do. Well, at least she can't tag along to the slumber party tonight."

As soon as Diane finished breakfast, she tried to sneak out. Maybe she could meet Lyn at the playground without having Trudy along. But Trudy guessed where Diane was headed.

"Can I go, too?" she asked Mom.

"Well, you can't go by yourself," Mom answered. "Will you take her, Diane? And see that she gets home okay?"

"Aw, Mommmm! Does Trudy always have to tag along?"

"She can play with her friends while you play with yours."

To Diane's surprise, it wasn't as bad as she thought. While she played volleyball, Trudy found some girls her own age. Soon they began climbing the monkey bars.

A few hours later Diane started home. As she and her friend Lyn walked together, Trudy fell behind.

Wondering what had happened to her, Diane looked back. Trudy had her head down, like she was looking for invisible footprints. What on earth was she doing?

"What's the matter?" asked Lyn, and Diane shrugged her shoulders.

Soon she felt curious and glanced back again. Trudy still walked strangely. Stretching out her legs, she took much bigger strides than usual. "Ah ha!" thought Diane. "She's trying to walk in my footsteps!"

Diane started walking as fast as she could. Lyn looked at her. "What are you . . .?"

Diane put her finger to her lips, whispered, "Shhhh," and tipped her head backward.

Lyn looked at Trudy and grinned. She, too, began

walking in long, giant strides. Still trying to stay in Diane's steps, Trudy started running. Soon she was gasping for breath.

Diane stopped, ready to say, "You're sure acting dumb, Trudy." But something inside Diane made her hold back the words. "Does she really care that much about being like me? Even in the way I walk?"

A moment later Diane was glad she hadn't said anything. As Lyn turned off for her own house, Trudy reached out for Diane's hand.

Diane looked down. For the first time she caught a glimpse of how much her little sister loved her. "It's kind of scary," Diane thought. "What if I do something to hurt her?" Somehow Trudy wasn't just a tagalong anymore.

When Diane and Trudy reached home, Mom met them in the kitchen. "I have a problem. Your dad and I are supposed to go to a concert tonight. Our babysitter just canceled. Do you know anyone who won't be going to your slumber party?"

Diane thought for a minute, then shook her head.

"I know what you can do with me," said Trudy. "I can go to the slumber party!"

"Mommmmmm!" Diane cried out. In that moment all of Diane's good feelings about Trudy disappeared.

Then, like a snapshot right in front of her, Diane remembered Trudy trying to walk in her footsteps. Instead of blurting out her feelings, she waited until her little sister went into the bathroom.

Then she drew a deep breath and plunged in, telling Mom how she felt.

TO TALK ABOUT

▶ Thought*less*ness tears relationships down. Thought*ful*ness builds them up. What are some thoughtful things Diane did in handling Trudy?
▶ When you live in a family, you sometimes need to give in and think about another person. Other times you need to explain why you feel the way you do. Which kind of time is this for Diane?
▶ When Diane explains how she feels about Trudy tagging along, she should tell two things: 1) what the problem is, and 2) how she feels about the problem. Pretend you're Diane. What would you say to her mom?
▶ What's the difference between Diane taking Trudy to the park and taking her to a slumber party?
▶ How will her friends feel about inviting Diane if she takes Trudy along everywhere she goes?
▶ When you talk about how you feel, you help your mom or dad understand things they may not have thought about. It also helps you feel better because you get your feelings out in the open. Things often don't seem as hard if you talk about them with the right person. What problems are you facing that

you'd like to talk about? A good way to begin is by saying, "I feel. . . ." Then finish the sentence, using feeling words like mad, or sad, or glad. If you have some ideas for solving the problem, be sure to mention those.

Be devoted to one another in brotherly love. Honor one another above yourselves. (Romans 12:10)

Help me, Lord, to be thoughtful about the feelings of others. Help me know when I should help someone else, and when I should explain what I need. Help our family to have good talks together.

JOEL'S HERO

Joel and his friend Ben were watching TV when Dad called from outside.

"Five more minutes, Dad," answered Joel. "Okay?"

But as the program ended, a newsflash caught and held him.

"Major league football player arrested for illegal possession of drugs. Arrested outside his home this morning, starting quarterback. . . ."

Joel jumped up, feeling like someone had kicked him in the stomach. "I don't believe it!"

But the newscaster went on, giving more details, then ending, "Update at five."

"That's awful," said Joel. "I can't believe Bart would take drugs."

"Hey, what's with you?" answered Ben. "Everybody's doing it."

"That's not true!"

"Sure it is! What's the big deal? My brother. . . ." Suddenly Ben stopped, as though remembering he wasn't supposed to say anything.

Joel turned off the TV. Ben headed home, and Joel went out to the back yard, dragging his feet the whole way.

Seeing him, Dad dropped a large log onto the wood splitter. Joel stood across from him and threw off the pieces that were the right size. When they needed to be split again, he pushed them back in against the wedge.

The woodpile grew higher, but Joel's mind wasn't on his work. The first time he let half a log fall off, Dad didn't say anything. The second time it happened, Joel caught Dad looking at him.

After that, Joel tried to think about what he was doing. Just the same, it wasn't long before he bumped a finger.

"Ow, ow, ow!" Pulling off his glove, Joel sucked the finger.

Dad stopped the splitter and sat down on a stump. "What's the matter, Joel? Besides your finger, I mean."

Joel dropped on the ground. "Aw, nothing," he said, turning his face away from Dad.

"Sure it is. Why don't you tell me about it?"

As Joel thought about the newsflash, he felt kicked in the stomach again. He felt so mixed up, he didn't think he could tell Dad about it.

But Dad asked once more, and Joel found himself talking. "Ben thinks it's okay—that everybody takes drugs. But it makes me mad! Bart's a football hero. I thought he was different!"

Joel's hurt and anger spilled out. "He came from here! When I was a little kid, he autographed my football."

"And you've had it on your shelf ever since. It hurts, doesn't it?"

Joel felt the tears at the back of his eyes and was glad Dad couldn't see his face.

"You believed in him. He made it to the big time."

Joel felt surprised that Dad understood. "I wanted. . . ." He broke off, afraid he'd sound dumb.

But Dad guessed. "You wanted to be like him when you grow up."

Joel nodded, still trying to hold the tears back. But they began streaming down his cheeks. He felt embarrassed and struggled to speak. "He was my hero—my hometown hero. . . ."

Dad reached out and put his hand on Joel's shoulder. "We need to be able to believe in people," he said. "But often they disappoint us, especially if we think they're perfect."

Joel pulled up the edge of his jacket and wiped his face. "But he's like one of us. If I can't believe in him. . . ."

"It hurts me too, Joel. I feel disappointed. I feel angry. I feel concerned for Bart. I wonder what happened that he decided to try something that would hurt him."

Dad squeezed Joel's shoulder and drew a deep breath. "When I was about your age, my basketball hero got drunk one Friday night. Our family went into town to shop, and I saw him staggering down the sidewalk."

Dad cleared his throat as though the memory still hurt. "Later on, something happened that bothered me even more. Maybe it sounds silly, but it wasn't to me. My Grandpa promised to take me fishing. I looked forward to it all week. I told all the kids at school. But Gramps got busy and forgot."

Something in Dad's voice caught Joel's attention. Joel turned to face him.

Dad took a deep breath. "And even though I don't want to, maybe I'll disappoint you sometime, too."

"But you're trying your best," said Joel. "And he was my idol. . . ."

"Your idol?"

"Yeah, my idol."

"It doesn't work to have idols, Joel. They might start meaning more to you than God."

After a long quiet moment, Dad stood up. "There's only one Person who will never disappoint you," he said.

Pulling on his work gloves, Joel stood up, too. He still hurt inside. Maybe he would for a long time. But he knew who that one Person was.

TO TALK ABOUT

▶Why is it important that we have people we can look up to? How can they help us grow and reach out to do hard things?

▶What mistake did Joel make in thinking about his hero?

▶What is an idol? What are some idols that people have?

▶Have you ever believed in someone and been badly disappointed? What happened?

▶Who is the one Person Joel's dad talked about? Why is He the only Person who will never disappoint you?

▶What responsibility do you have to people who like and respect you?

"*Whoever believes in [Jesus] will not be disappointed.*" (Romans 10:11, GNB)

Jesus, I hurt inside when I like someone and find out they aren't as great as I thought. Thanks that I can look to You, and You'll never disappoint me.

WE'RE
THE BEST!

Tanya woke to a stream of sunlight coming through the window. For a moment she didn't know where she was. Then she remembered—Dad's new house.

In the other bed, Lori still slept. "She'd be nice," thought Tanya. "That is, if she didn't have to be my sister."

Tanya wished there wasn't a Lori. She wished there weren't two younger brothers. Most of all, she wished there wasn't Lori's mom, Darlene.

Tanya closed her eyes and tried to go back to sleep. Instead, she remembered how she felt about leaving Mom for this weekend with Dad's new family.

"The divorce is something between Dad and me,"

123

Mom had told her. "I don't like it any more than you do. But he's your father. You can love me and still have a good relationship with him."

Instead Tanya felt mad—mad that there'd been a divorce. She felt jealous that Lori and the others got to be with Dad all the time. Even worse, Tanya felt lonely and afraid and wished Mom was here.

"Are they going to leave me out?" she wondered. "Or will they act nice to me because they think they have to?"

Lori stirred, and the day began. Around the breakfast table, Dad brought out new T-shirts he'd bought. A bright red, they had bold blue letters across the front—letters that said, WE'RE THE BUTTERFIELDS. Across the back were more words: WE'RE THE BEST!

Tanya looked at Lori and could tell she liked the shirts. With a whoop, her two little brothers tore off the shirts they were wearing and pulled on the new ones. Darlene smiled quietly at Dad, and Dad smiled back.

Inside, Tanya felt terrible. She remembered when she was Dad's only kid. "Do I still count with him? Does he still love me?" she wondered. Then she thought of Mom, sitting alone at home. Wearing the shirt seemed disloyal to her.

"Let's get 'em on, and go for a hike," said Dad.

Tanya jumped up, glad to get away from the table. But she moved slowly up the stairs. Even more slowly, she shut the door to the room she and Lori shared.

Glad that Lori hadn't followed her, Tanya sat down on the floor. She felt mad and sad all at once.

"I don't wanna wear it," she thought. "I'm not a Butterfield. Sure, that's my name. But I'm not part of *this* family."

For a long time she sat there, unwilling to move. Then someone knocked on the door. "Hey, Tanya!" Dad called out.

Tanya didn't answer, and Dad called again. Finally she stood up and opened the door.

"We're all ready. Let's go," said Dad. Then he saw Tanya's face. "What's the matter?"

Tanya made herself look at Dad. "I don't want to wear the shirt."

Just in time she caught the hurt look in his eyes. "I've got a new life, chicken. I want you to be part of it."

"But. . . ." Tanya wished he wouldn't call her chicken. That was for then, back when she was little. Back when he and Mom lived together and they gave her a baby chicken for Easter.

Tanya looked down.

"You're worried about your mother, aren't you?" asked Dad.

Slowly Tanya nodded.

"Why don't we call this a special shirt? Wear it on weekends when you're with us. Just leave it here when you go home."

125

Still Tanya stared at the floor.

"I love you, chicken," he said softly. "You belong here, too, you know."

Dad gave her a quick hug, then started toward the stairs. "We'll be waiting in the car for you."

When he left, Tanya picked up the shirt, and looked once more at the lettering. With her finger she traced the B, then the U, then the whole name. "I love you, Mom," she whispered.

But then, as clearly as if Mom were there, Tanya remembered her words. "He's your father. You can love me and still have a good relationship with him."

Tanya turned over the shirt. Through the blur of tears, WE'RE THE BEST! stared up at her.

Blinking the tears away, she remembered Dad at the breakfast table. "I guess I have to think about his feelings, too."

Tanya drew a deep breath. "Maybe I've gotta give up the idea of one family. Guess I'm part of two families now."

In that moment she made a choice. Slowly she pulled on the shirt. "Maybe someday I'll even feel like I belong."

TO TALK ABOUT

▶What does it mean to be loyal to someone? Why is loyalty a good quality to have?

▶Why did Tanya's feelings of loyalty make it hard for her when her parents were divorced? What idea helped her work out her problem?

▶Because her dad had a new family, Tanya wondered if he still loved her. For him—and for all of us—it's possible to love more than one person at a time. Even though a dad or mom remarries, it usually doesn't change the love they have for their children. How do you know Tanya's father loves her?

▶Who is with Tanya, no matter where she lives? How do you know?

▶Often you'll make choices that make a difference in what happens to you. But it's not possible to control *everything* that happens. In those times, what counts is what you do about the hard things you can't change. In what way do you need to know God is with you? How can He help you with your problems?

The LORD said, "So do not fear, for I am with you; do not be dismayed, for I am your God. I will strengthen you and help you; I will uphold you with my right-eous right hand." (Isaiah 41:10)

Thank You, God, for the parents You've given me. Show me how to have a good relationship with both of them. Thank You that wherever I live, You are with me.

128

BUFFY AND THE GAME

When Mom started a new job with different hours, Todd didn't like it one bit. Now he had to do all kinds of things he never did before.

"Be sure to take Buffy out before you go to school," Mom said as she left for work.

"Aw, Mom," Todd answered. "Have Mark do it. He's older."

"I've asked Mark to do other things. You're in charge of Buffy."

Usually Todd liked the little cocker spaniel. He'd taught her to fetch sticks, speak for a treat, play dead, and hold out a paw to shake hands. Whenever Todd came home from school, Buffy waited at the door, wagging her tail in welcome.

Often she seemed to sense if Todd was happy or sad. Once Todd was sick for two weeks and couldn't stand it any longer. Buffy jumped up on the bed. Rolling over on the spread, she played dead. Then she licked Todd's face until he laughed.

But now Todd was older. He had plenty of other things to do. Sometimes Buffy seemed like too much work.

Taking hold of Buffy's collar, Todd opened the back door. As he hooked her to the chain, a blast of cold air whipped through his hair. Todd shivered and shut the door. Going into the family room, he plopped down in front of the TV.

As he caught the sports news, he called out to Mark. "Hey! The Rangers won!"

Mark stuck his head in the door. "I know. And Dad bought tickets for tomorrow night's game!"

"For all of us?" asked Todd. Hockey was his favorite sport.

"Yep. All of us."

Twenty minutes later, Mark looked in again. "Hey, aren't you ready?" He zipped up his jacket. "I'm going. I don't want to miss the bus."

Todd jumped up, grabbed his books and jacket, and headed out the front door. As he ran after Mark, the winter air stung his cheeks. The bus was half a block away, but he made it.

When Todd and Mark returned home that after-noon, something seemed strange. At first the house just seemed quieter than usual. But as they headed to the kitchen for peanut butter toast, he and Mark heard Buffy bark.

"She's outside?" asked Mark. "You didn't bring her in?"

Todd hurried to the back door. Buffy was so glad to see him, she jumped all over him and licked his hands before bounding into the warm house. Feeling guilty, Todd rolled on the floor, playing with her.

But Mark was angry. "She's a house dog. She's not used to being outside all day."

"Aw, bug off," said Todd. "Nothing happened. She's okay."

"If she lived in a doghouse, she'd have a thick coat. But she hasn't. It's too cold to be outside so long."

"Hey, get off my back."

"She probably barked all day."

"I said, 'Bug off!'" snapped Todd. "Now do it."

"No, I won't," said Mark. "I'm gonna tell Mom when she gets home."

"You do, and I'll say it's all your fault. You didn't tell me it was time for the bus. That's why I forgot Buffy."

"I'm not *supposed* to tell you," said Mark. "You can read the clock."

All evening the little dog shivered. When Todd

went to bed, he covered Buffy with a blanket and hoped Mom wouldn't notice. But the next morning Buffy's eyes were matted. Every now and then she wheezed. As she looked at Todd, she whimpered.

Todd felt scared, yet he wondered, "How can I pin the blame on Mark? If Mom and Dad find out, they'll ground me. I won't get to see the Rangers."

"This dog is sick," said Mom. "What happened?"

"It's Mark's fault," answered Todd.

"No, it's not!" said Mark. "It's your fault, and you know it!"

"Mommmm! He's lying! I did some work for him, and he promised to take Buffy in."

"You're the liar! I can't believe the way you make

up a story! You just don't wanna get in trouble!"

Mom looked from one to the other. Todd looked her straight in the eye.

Inside, he felt terrible. He knew he wasn't telling the truth. Yet if he explained what really happened, Mom wouldn't let him go to the game.

Todd leaned down and started petting Buffy.

TO TALK ABOUT

▶How do you feel about what Todd did to Buffy?

▶When Todd started doing something wrong, how did one thing build on top of another?

▶What do you think Todd's mom should say? Do you think Todd will go to the game?

▶What will happen to Todd if he gets away with lying and blaming someone else when he's in trouble?

▶How will Todd's lie hurt his relationship with Mark?

▶If you've lied about something, what's the best way to correct the lie? How do you know?

No temptation has seized you except what is common to man. And God is faithful; he will not let you be tempted beyond what you can bear. But when you are tempted, he will also provide a way out so that you can stand up under it. (1 Corinthians 10:13)

Help me, Jesus, when I'm tempted to lie and put the blame on others. I want to be honest with You, with others, and with myself. Thanks that You'll give me the strength to tell the truth.

JILL RETURNS HOME

"**Y**our family wants *me* to go skiing with them?" asked Jill.

"Sure," said Cathy. "Why not?"

"I've never been before. I don't know how." She didn't want to tell Cathy her family never did anything like that.

"That doesn't matter," said Cathy. "We'll teach you. It's not hard to learn to cross-country ski."

Inside, Jill felt scared. "What if I can't do it?" Yet she kept pushing the thought aside. Every part of her wanted to try.

Aloud she asked, "You're *sure* your mom and dad want me along?"

"Yep," answered Cathy. "When we go for a week-

135

end, they always let me take a friend. You're my first choice. Okay?"

"Okay!" But Jill's thoughts raced off to her own family. "I can't imagine Mom and Dad wanting me along." When they went someplace, it was usually a bar. They always left her and her older brother at home.

Cathy broke into her thoughts. "We'll leave right after school on Friday and rent skis for you when we get there. Okay?"

"Okay," Jill echoed again.

And so, it was all set. A week later Jill, Cathy, and her mom and dad found an open space near the beginning of the ski trail.

"Slide your foot in like this," said Mrs. Sullivan. "Take your pole and push down the lock."

Mr. Sullivan showed Jill the best way to move ahead. "You kick one ski backward and glide forward on the other." Soon Jill got the hang of it.

"Sandra and I will take off first," said Mr. Sullivan. "We'll stop every now and then to make sure you're getting along okay." Jabbing their ski poles into the snow, Cathy's mom and dad started down the trail.

"You're next," said Cathy, and Jill took her place at the top of the slope. "Just dig in your poles and push."

The winding trail led off through the woods. It wasn't long before Jill felt at home on skis. She even managed the small hills without falling down very often. By the time she started getting tired, Jill decided skiing was the most fun she'd ever had.

Rounding a bend, she saw Cathy's parents at the side of the trail. They'd brushed snow off a picnic table, and Mrs. Sullivan was taking food from her backpack. "Winter picnic!" she called.

Jill unsnapped her skis and dropped onto the bench. As she saw the sandwiches and apples, her stomach growled. But just as she reached out, ready to dive in, every head bowed.

Every head except Jill's. She felt uncomfortable. As she watched, Cathy and her parents began praying.

"What a creepy thing to do," Jill thought. Yet it seemed to mean something to them. Jill closed her eyes, so they wouldn't catch her staring. "Is that what makes them different?"

When everyone started skiing again, Jill asked Cathy, "How come your family has fun together?"

"What do you mean?"

"You're different."

Cathy hooted, as though she wasn't sure how to take that. "We're different all right."

"You are. You're nice to each other. How come?"

Cathy's grin faded, and her eyes were serious. "We haven't always been that way."

"Then what happened?"

"First Mom became a Christian. Then I did. Then

we prayed for Dad. We prayed a lon-n-ng time."

As they followed the ski trail, Jill was quiet, thinking about it. "Would that work with my family? They'd probably just laugh at the whole thing."

Twilight soon fell on the woods, and they needed to stop skiing. When they began again the next morning, Jill still watched all the Sullivans.

"I wish. . . ." A thought started to take shape. All day the longing grew inside her. She wanted something more in her life. She wanted more for her family.

Off and on Jill asked Cathy questions. She discovered Jesus loved her, the way He loved the Sullivans. On Saturday night Jill asked Jesus to be her Savior and Lord.

When the Sullivans brought her home on Sunday afternoon, Jill knew the hard part was ahead. "I want my family to know Jesus," she thought. Yet she felt more scared than when she'd faced her first big hill on skis.

As she sat down for supper, Jill looked around the table. Her brother Nick reached across for a roll. Mom helped herself to potatoes, and Dad dug in.

Wondering if they could hear her heart pound, Jill bowed her head. Silently she offered the prayer she learned from the Sullivans. Looking up, Jill saw Nick staring at her.

"What's with you? Did you get religion over the weekend?"

Jill felt the warm flush of embarrassment reach her cheeks. "Yes, I did," she said quietly. She wondered if her heart could pound right out of her chest.

"What are you, a Jesus freak or something?" asked Nick, his voice scornful.

Mom jumped in. "Now, Jill, we don't want you getting caught up in something that won't be good for you."

Jill swallowed hard and wondered if she should bail out. "Should I pretend nothing happened to me? Will they ever understand?" Yet she knew the choice she'd made was something real.

Then Jill saw the look in Dad's eyes. "He's listening. Maybe I'll have to pray for a long time. But he's listening."

In spite of the way Nick poked fun at her, Jill began to explain.

TO TALK ABOUT

▶What made Jill want what Cathy's family had?

▶What did Jill learn about what God is like by watching the Sullivans?

▶What do you think would happen to Jill's family if she *didn't* explain about her salvation?

▶Jesus promised that the Holy Spirit would be our Helper. How can the Holy Spirit help Jill tell her family about Jesus?

▶Has there been a time when the Holy Spirit helped you talk to someone who didn't know Jesus? What happened?

Jesus said, "Go back home to your family and tell them how much the LORD has done for you and how kind he has been to you." (Mark 5:19, GNB)

Jesus, I'm often too scared to tell the people close to me about You. Yet I know You want me to. Give me all the power of Your Holy Spirit to help. Thank You!

IN THE MIDDLE OF THE NIGHT

As Danny ran down the alley, he felt the night press in. The footsteps behind him moved more quickly. Whoever it was no longer tried to be quiet. Closer and closer the footsteps came.

With all the strength he had, Danny rushed ahead. His heart pounded as loud as the footsteps. If only he could reach home. . . . If only he could get inside the door. . . .

Somehow he'd missed the way. Danny looked around, searching for something he knew. Instead, the buildings on either side seemed to close in on him.

As he came to the end of the alley, he gasped. It was a dead end! He couldn't escape!

Just then Danny felt a hand grab his shoulder. He

141

hit out, trying to push the person away. Instead, the hand held on and kept shaking him. Then he heard a familiar voice.

"Danny! Danny! Wake up!"

As he opened his eyes, Danny felt surprised. In the dream he'd been back in his own country. The old streets still seemed real. But now soft light streamed into his bedroom from the hallway. His new mom sat on the edge of the bed.

"What's the matter, Danny?"

The night was still in his spirit, the alleyway too close. He was afraid to talk about it, afraid to admit how scared he'd been. "Nothing," he said.

"Yes there is. Night after night you have terrible dreams. I don't think they'll stop until we talk about them."

But Danny wasn't ready.

"Did you watch something scary on TV when we were gone this evening?"

Danny shook his head.

"Did you read a scary book?"

Again Danny shook his head. Finally Mom kissed his forehead and went back to bed.

As soon as Danny fell back asleep, he had another nightmare. He woke up moaning, and the sobs began. When Mom and Dad came into his room, he tried to stop crying, but couldn't.

Dad sat down on one side of the bed and put his

hand on Danny's head. "Something must have happened to you before you came to this country. Do you remember what it was?"

Slowly Danny nodded as the tears streamed down his cheeks.

"Can you tell us about it?"

Danny shook his head.

"Why don't you tell us what you're dreaming?" asked Mom.

"I can't remember it all," he answered, still afraid to admit how scared he felt.

"Just tell us the parts you do remember," said Dad. "Maybe you're having the same nightmare over and over."

Danny pulled up the quilt and settled deeper into bed. "Someone always chases me. It's always dark. I keep trying to find our house, but I never can. It's never in the right place." The tears began again, and it was a long time before they stopped.

Finally Dad spoke. "Danny, when you first came to our family, you didn't know enough English to tell us about your parents. Can you tell us now?"

It was buried so deep Danny wasn't sure he could talk about it. But Dad waited, and finally the words stumbled out. "One day Mom and Dad were there. The next day they weren't. They left me."

Danny started to shiver, in spite of the blankets around him. "I cried and cried until someone came."

As Danny looked up, he saw tears in Mom's eyes.

"That's why you're afraid, isn't it?" she asked. "That's why you keep having nightmares."

Danny nodded, but there was something else. Danny was afraid to say it, afraid that if he did, it might happen.

Just the same, Mom guessed. "Danny, are you afraid something will happen to us? Are you afraid we'll leave you?"

Danny's gaze never left Mom's face, but his smallest voice said yes.

Mom leaned forward and took Danny's hand. "There's a verse in the Bible that says God puts the lonely in families (Psalm 68:6). Let's ask God to help us take care of you. Okay?"

Danny wasn't sure he wanted to be prayed for, but he knew Mom and Dad would do it anyway. In a secret place in his heart he felt kind of glad. More than anything, he wanted to believe the words in the Bible were true.

"Jesus, help Danny know You'll take care of him. Give him the faith to believe what You've promised," asked Dad.

"And Jesus, we ask You to heal Danny," said Mom. "Fill him with Your love, way down deep in his feelings and mind."

In that moment, something deep within Danny reached up to Jesus. He couldn't explain it, but all of

his hurt and scared feelings seemed to fall away.
Now he felt peaceful, deep inside.

TO TALK ABOUT

▶What does it mean to feel peaceful? Who has promised to give us peace? (For clues see John 14:27.)

▶When Jesus heals Danny's mind and feelings, he will still remember that his birth parents left him. But when he thinks about it, he probably won't hurt anymore. What do you suppose will happen to Danny's nightmares?

▶Can you think of a time when Jesus helped you feel better about something that hurt or scared you? What happened? In what way did you know Jesus loves you?

▶Both of Danny's parents left him. But some children feel hurt because a mom or dad left home instead of staying married. Has that happened to you, or to someone you know? Why is it important to talk about your feelings with the parent you live with?

▶In what ways does God take care of you? Why can you always count on Jesus being with you?

Jesus said, "Surely I am with you always, to the very end of the age." (Matthew 28:20)

Thank You, Jesus, that You've promised to be with me forever. I ask You to heal me where I hurt. Thanks for loving me. Thanks that I can count on You to take care of me.

THE REAL WINNER

Captain for the Js, Janie crouched, ready for the jump. If there was anyone in the world she wanted to beat, it was Carla, captain of the Cs. No matter what Carla did, she always won. Janie's feelings about beating her went far beyond a game in gym class.

Once in a while Janie wished she could be Carla's friend. But most of the time, Janie just wanted to prove she could do something better. Now, as she faced Carla, their gym teacher, Miss Macklin, held up the basketball.

"How you play is more important than winning," Mackey often said. "People are more important than points."

But Janie just wanted to win. As the whistle blew, she leapt high in the air, tipping the ball to her teammate Liz. Liz dribbled her way out of a tight spot and moved down the court. Janie slipped under the basket and waited for the ball. When it came, she managed a jump shot.

Swish! It went in!

The Js cheered, but the Cs looked ready to fight every step of the way. It was their ball.

Standing at the end of the court, Carla looked around. Spotting a break in the Js defense, she threw the ball in. Her teammate caught it, and headed toward the basket. Then the ball returned to Carla. Her long shot bounced on the board, but dropped in.

Back and forth the score jumped with one side leading, then the other. At the half the score was tied, 24-24. Janie knew the game would be hard fought to the end. Facing Carla was always tough.

"I'm just as good a player," Janie told herself. "But I always seem to lose."

With only a few minutes left in the final quarter, the score was 40-38, the Js ahead. "If only we can keep it," thought Janie, aching with the desire to win.

Muscles tense, she guarded Carla closely. Swinging her arms up and down, Janie tried to block a pass to the Cs. Then, as Carla started in for a basket, Janie grabbed the ball.

The whistle blew. "Foul!"

Janie groaned. Carla moved to the free throw line. Her first try fell short. Janie breathed deep. But the second one dropped in. 40-39, with the Js leading by only one point.

As the ball went into play, Janie's team caught it and started moving toward their own basket. Liz passed the ball to Janie. Carla leapt high and intercepted. In the same moment she lost her footing and landed on the floor. The ball spun out of her hands.

Janie grabbed for it. Just before the ball rolled out of bounds, she touched it.

Mackey's whistle shrilled. "Js out!"

Janie looked back, surprised at the call. Had Carla's body blocked Mackey's view? Janie knew she didn't have the right to take the ball, but Mackey hadn't seen her touch it.

In that split second, Janie's thoughts jumped ahead. Having the ball now could make the difference between winning and losing. "Carla was on her back. She didn't see," Janie told herself. "No one will know."

As she picked up the basketball, Janie saw Carla look at her. She wondered if Carla knew. "If she did, she'd say something," Janie told herself. "I can get by with it."

She walked to the sideline, and Mackey joined her there. Janie waited for the whistle that would send the ball into play. "If we can keep it one minute, we'll win," she thought.

But as Janie stood there, she remembered Mackey's favorite saying. "People are more important than points."

Once more Janie debated with herself, unsure what to do. A knot formed in the pit of her stomach. "We're almost there," she thought. "We can win. But what if we beat Carla, and I know it wasn't fair?"

Her feelings weren't in it, but Janie turned to Mackey. "I don't think I should have the ball. I touched it just before it went out."

Mackey looked surprised, but signaled for Carla to take Janie's place. Carla threw the ball out, and everyone snapped into action. Janie kept close, but suddenly Carla broke loose. One of the Cs passed her the ball.

Instantly Carla took a long shot. Just as it went in, the final whistle blew. 40-41! The Cs had won the game.

Janie's shoulders slumped. "By *one* point," she groaned. As soon as she could, Janie headed for the locker room and a bench in an out-of-the way corner. She didn't want to talk with anyone.

But Liz found her there. "How come you told Mackey? We would have won."

Janie couldn't answer. She felt mad at herself. Mad for being honest. She had almost tasted victory, then she'd let it slip out of her hands.

"No one would have known," said Liz.

"I know," answered Janie.

Just then she heard a voice behind her. "I would have," said Carla. "As I rolled over, I saw Janie touch the ball. I would've said something. I was waiting to see what she'd do."

As Janie turned, she looked straight into Carla's eyes and felt glad that she could.

"You played a good game, Janie." Carla held out her hand.

Janie grasped it. "You played a good game, too," she said, feeling surprised that she meant it.

Carla grinned. "When we start playing other schools, we'll be on the same team."

As she saw something new in Carla's eyes, Janie felt warm all the way though. "Maybe . . ." she thought. "Maybe we'll even be friends."

TO TALK ABOUT

▶ It was hard for Janie to be honest. Then she lost the game besides. Why is it important to be honest, even when things don't seem to turn out right?

▶ In sports it's easy to think, "Win, no matter what you have to do." How would Janie have felt if she'd beaten Carla unfairly? How would it make her feel about having a friendship with Carla?

▶ If Janie had been unfair, how would Carla have felt about being friends? Why?

▶Have you ever had a friend you couldn't trust? What happened to your friendship?

▶Why does it seem that a friend who is fair is someone cheering for you?

▶Why do you think this story is called "The Real Winner"? Who really won in the end? In what way?

Even a child shows what he is by what he does; you can tell if he is honest and good. (Proverbs 20:11, GNB)

Jesus, I want to be someone people can count on. Help me to be honest and play fair. Help me do what's right, even when You're the only One who knows. Thank You!

152

LONG
BUS RIDE

Gary rolled onto his stomach and pulled the blankets over his head. Even so, he could hear Mom's voice.

"Garrrrry! Time to get up!"

Gary groaned, and a moment later fell back asleep. He woke to Mom's hand on his shoulder. "Gary! Gary! Wake up!"

Slowly his eyes came open. Rubbing them, Gary yawned. He didn't like getting up in the morning. He'd much rather stay up nights and sleep late.

Finally Gary sat up, and Mom left the room. "Friday," he thought. "Well, at least tomorrow's Saturday. No school."

But then Gary thought about the bus ride to

school. His stomach muscles tightened.

Forty-five minutes later he climbed aboard. This was the moment he dreaded, and there was no way of getting around it.

"Hey, Gary!" Kurt called out from the back of the bus. "Sit here!"

Gary shook his head and looked for a seat near the front.

"What's the matter, Gary? You chicken?" yelled another boy. "We're saving you a place."

This time Gary forced a smile and answered. If he didn't, they'd bug him the whole ride. "Nah, I like the scenery up here."

Dropping into an empty seat, he faced the front and pretended he didn't hear the answer. But on the inside Gary hurt.

"When will they stop?" he wondered. "Every morning, every afternoon. . . ."

The boys who usually got in trouble sat in the back of the bus. When school started that fall, Gary sat with them. Then one day they started passing drugs. Gary decided he'd had enough.

The next morning he sat farther forward in the bus. But since then the kids hadn't let up.

"I know I'm right," Gary told himself. "But it sure is hard sticking to it."

Most of the kids sitting near the front were younger than Gary. He felt almost as uncomfortable with them as with the boys at the back.

Once again Kurt called out to him. Others joined in. Trying to pretend he didn't hear, Gary stared out the window.

"I'll beat 'em at their own game," he thought. "Who cares? I can make it on my own." Yet he wasn't sure he meant it.

As the bus stopped in front of school, Gary stood up, eager to get away from the other boys. But Kurt pushed forward, blocked the aisle ahead of Gary, and turned to glare at him.

Gary stepped into the aisle, but stayed far enough back so Kurt couldn't kick him. Whatever Kurt tried to do, it was always sneaky enough so the bus driver couldn't see.

But as Gary waited for the aisle to clear, Kurt's best friend moved up behind Gary. Gary felt cold shivers running down his spine. "What're they planning?" he wondered.

He knew he could fight. He'd done it before. But he'd be taking on more than Kurt, and he felt scared. "I can't fight 'em all."

In that split-second Gary faced the truth. "I *can't* do it alone. If they beat me up again, I might give in."

Gary hated the idea. He didn't want the guys to win. At the same time he was afraid. So afraid that he silently prayed three words: "Help me, Jesus."

In that instant something changed inside Gary.

He straightened up, and stood his tallest.

Outwardly everything seemed the same. Kurt and his friend still hemmed him in. Kurt still stared at Gary. But this time Gary stared back without looking away.

In that moment the bus driver saw Kurt in the mirror. "Hey, get moving!"

When Monday morning dawned the next week, Gary got up before his mother called him. No matter how much he wanted to sleep, he turned on his light.

There, where no one could see what he was doing, he took out his Bible. "Help me, Jesus," he asked. "Just help me get through the day."

Gary began to read. It was strange how much better he felt after just a few verses. Then, as he prayed about what to do, he had an idea—an idea he'd had before. But up until now he'd always told himself NO!

That morning at breakfast, Gary told Mom about his long bus rides.

TO TALK ABOUT

▶What important choices did Gary make?
▶What is the difference between saying no like you mean it, and saying no as though you're half scared? Give an example. Why do tougher kids pick on kids who seem scared?
▶Have you ever had to say NO to some other kids?

What happened when you did?

▶What's the difference between squealing on some-one and knowing when it's time to ask the right person for help? How can Gary's mom help him without other kids knowing about it?

▶Gary started reading his Bible because he had a big need. If you're like Gary, it helps to pray, "Jesus, what do You want me to know about . . . ?" (Tell Jesus what your special need is.) Begin reading in the Bible and stop when a verse seems real, as though it fits what's happening to you. If you read the Bible every day, you'll know when the Holy Spirit helps you. Words seem to jump off the page. Have you had times when the Bible seemed very real to you? What happened?

▶Is there a verse that helped you face something hard? What is it?

▶If you don't have a Bible, ask your mom or dad, or someone else who can give you one. If you haven't read the Bible before, you might like to start with the Gospel of John, the fourth book in the New Testa-ment. Look in the contents at the beginning of the Bible, and you'll find it.

Moses said, "Don't be afraid! Stand your ground, and you will see what the LORD will do to save you today." (Exodus 14:13, GNB)

Jesus, I'm afraid. Help me to be strong and not give in to wrong things. Show me what to do about the things that make me scared. Thank You that talking with Mom or Dad is always a good choice.

THROW-AWAY FRIEND

"Thanks, Dad," Christy said, as she climbed out of the car. Her best friend Sara said goodbye and followed Christy.

Standing on the sidewalk, they looked up at the large SKATELAND sign. Both of them liked to roller-skate. All week they'd looked forward to Saturday afternoon.

Minutes later Christy and Sara tied the laces on their skates and stood up. It was still early, but filling up fast. As they moved into the flow of skaters, Christy edged toward the middle. She wanted to practice some new turns before the rink got crowded.

She was beginning to feel good about her moves when she heard someone call her name. Looking up, she saw Annette, a girl from her class at school.

"Hey, this is gonna be great!" thought Christy, waving back. Annette and her friends were the most popular kids in the class.

Last year Annette had been class president. She always managed to be in the middle of anything fun. Being Annette's friend was a sure ticket to being popular.

"What can I do to get in with her?" Christy wondered. "At least I look good on skates. Maybe Annette will notice."

She did. When the group skating stopped, Annette came over to where Christy and Sara waited on the sidelines.

"You're a good skater, Christy," said Annette, not seeming to notice Sara.

Just then a special skate was called. "Triples," said Annette to Christy. "Why don't we ask Jon?"

Christy felt like she'd received an extra bonus. She'd had a secret crush on Jon for two years. "Skate with him?" she thought. "I'll jump at the chance!"

The afternoon began to seem like a once-in-a-lifetime dream. Annette or one of her friends got Christy into each of the special skates. She barely noticed how often Sara sat on the sidelines.

When the manager announced boy's choice, Jon skated up to Christy. "Wow!" she thought. "He's really asking me!"

As they skated away, Christy saw Sara's face. She seemed to have put on a mask, but for a moment the mask slipped. Sara's eyes looked hurt.

With a jolt, Christy realized she'd been so busy with the other kids she'd forgotten Sara. In fact, she hadn't brought her into a single skate.

As she and Jon moved away, Christy once again forgot Sara. Jon was a good skater, and it was easy to keep in step. Soon they were laughing together. "He's as much fun as Sara," thought Christy.

In that moment a twinge of uneasiness shot through her. There it was again—Sara. Rounding a corner, Christy saw her sitting on the bench by herself.

161

When the couple's skate ended, Christy skated up to her. "Do you want a candy bar?" she asked.

Sara jumped up, acting as if nothing had come between them. And somehow Christy found it a relief to be with Sara. "I don't have to impress her," thought Christy. "She's just like she always is—my friend."

When they finished their candy, Christy and Sara went back on the floor. Again Christy headed for the middle and started skating backwards.

Annette found her there. "The kids are coming over to my house for supper," she said. "Want to come along?"

"Do I want to!" thought Christy. "That isn't hard to decide." She started to say yes, then remembered Sara.

"Sara and I came together. Can she come, too?"

A strange look crossed Annette's face. "Well, uh. . . ."

For a moment she stood there, and Christy guessed. Annette didn't want to say no, but she didn't want to say yes either.

"Who's picking you up?" asked Annette.

"My dad," said Christy.

"Why don't you take Sara home, then have your dad drop you off at my place?"

Christy was tempted. More than anything she wanted to go to Annette's. More than anything she wanted to be part of their group. But Christy felt

162

uneasy again. In that moment she knew what was wrong. "Am I throwing away Sara the minute someone else comes along?"

Christy knew what her answer should be, but the world seemed to crash around her. "Will Annette ever invite me again?" She wished Annette hadn't forced her to make a choice.

But when she spoke she said, "I'm sorry. I'd like to come, but Sara's my friend."

Annette shrugged her shoulders and skated away, and Christy watched her go.

TO TALK ABOUT

▶As we grow and change, our friends may change over time. How is that different from what happened between Christy and Sara?

▶It looked like it would be better for Christy to become friends with Annette. What do you think?

▶We live in a world of throwaways—pop bottles, tin cans, paper plates. What does it mean to have throwaway friends?

▶What would happen to Christy if she always chose her friends based on who seemed popular at the moment?

▶How would Sara feel if she found out Christy took her home, then went to Annette's? How would Christy feel about herself if she did that to Sara?

▶In the Bible we read about the friendship between David and Jonathan (1 Samuel 20). How was their friendship tested?

▶What does the word *loyal* mean? How did Jonathan and David stay loyal to one another?

▶Think about the friends you have. In what ways do you feel loyal to them? Are there ways they've been loyal to you?

Some friendships do not last, but some friends are more loyal than brothers. (Proverbs 18:24, GNB)

Jesus, You've given me some special friends. Help me be loyal, so I don't throw them away whenever there's someone more popular. Thanks for being my best Friend. I want most of all to be loyal to You.

ON EAGLES' WINGS

On that February morn-
ing, snow still covered the northern Wisconsin ground.
Chip looked out the window and wished the school
day was over. He didn't want to give a science report.
He felt scared all the way through.

Besides, the room was hot and stuffy. Chip rolled
up the sleeves of his plaid flannel shirt and started
thinking about what he'd do when he got home.

Just then his science teacher called on him. Chip
slowly stood up. He hated giving speeches. In fact, he
hated everything about school. No matter what he did,
he seemed to get in trouble. But today he was going to
talk about bald eagles.

When Chip reached the front, he shifted from one

foot to the other, wondering where to begin. "Eagles have big nests," he said finally, afraid to look at the kids. Then, as he thought about the eagles, some of his fear dropped away. "Their nests can be six to eight feet across and almost that deep."

Just then a boy in the front row snickered and looked at Rob, Chip's neighbor and friend. Rob shook his head. But the boy snickered again.

"One really big nest weighed two tons," said Chip. In that moment a girl in the same row covered her mouth with her hand, as though trying to keep from laughing. "What's so funny?" wondered Chip.

Whatever it was seemed to be catching. A boy at the back of the room poked another kid, then looked at Chip. Chip's friend Rob was trying to keep his face straight.

"A pair of eagles usually goes back to the same nest every year," Chip said. Though he knew what he was talking about, his voice was beginning to sound uncertain. "Eagles sometimes get to be fifty years old."

Over near the window a girl giggled. "What am I saying wrong?" wondered Chip, struggling to keep on.

"Young bald eagles look like hawks. They get their white head and tail feathers when they're about four years old."

Again the girl giggled but even louder, and the boy next to her snickered. Chip swallowed hard. "It's something about me," he thought. He felt the red hot flush of embarrassment flood into his face.

Once more he tried to speak, but this time nothing came out. Suddenly he gave up. Going back to his desk, he dropped into the seat.

"Did you finish, Chip?" asked the teacher.

Chip hadn't finished. He could tell much more. But he nodded his head, afraid to speak. "I'll get a lousy grade anyway," he told himself. "I always do. I'll never give a speech again!"

He felt miserable. "How come they laughed at me?" Not wanting to see the grins on their faces, Chip looked down. Suddenly he realized what was wrong. That morning he'd missed a button on his flannel shirt. As he stood in front of the class, the bottom of the shirt had been shorter on one side than the other.

Once again Chip felt the hot blood go to his face. He felt silly all the way through. The kids would never let him forget—that is, unless he beat them up.

It seemed the day would never end, but finally Chip was on the school bus going home. When it ground to a halt, Chip and Rob climbed down together. Chip's house was at the end of a long dirt road back in the woods. Rob's family lived on the same road, but closer to the highway.

Sometimes Rob seemed like Chip's best buddy. Other times Chip couldn't stand him. Today their fight started the minute they got off the bus.

"Why didn't you back me up?" asked Chip. "You

coulda told the driver it wasn't my fault."

"But it was," said Rob. "You picked on Tommy, and I'm not gonna lie about it. Just like I'm not gonna lie about your fight on the playground today."

"That wasn't my fault either," said Chip, unwilling to tell Rob he'd beaten up a kid who laughed at him.

"Oh, yeah? Like it wasn't your fault when you went squirrel hunting and shot the windows out of old man Bailey's barn."

Chip bent down, picked up some snow and started shaping a ball.

"Like it wasn't your fault that you swiped a can of gas last night."

Suddenly Chip looked up.

"Saw you comin' out of our shed," said Rob. "I was upstairs and it was dark, but I just happened to look out. Why'd you want it anyway? Were you going snowmobiling?"

Chip bent down for more snow.

"If you'd asked, Mom woulda given it to you. Why didn't you ask?"

"Aw, get off my back," said Chip, but his thoughts kept running on. Sure he'd taken the gas. Why not? But right now he didn't want Rob snitching on him.

It wouldn't be so bad if Rob was just good in school. But he was good in everything. He could hunt and fish and trap, and even played the guitar.

168

More than once Chip had given him a bloody nose to set things straight between them. Now Chip felt uneasy. "If he tells his ma, she'll tell my ma. Maybe I should beat him up, just to make sure."

As though reading Chip's thoughts, Rob started to run, staying out of Chip's reach. Chip lobbed the snowball in his direction. Rob ducked and headed into his yard. When Rob's mom looked out the kitchen window, Chip knew he'd better not try again.

Walking on, he soon left the dirt road. The snow was deep in the woods, but Chip followed a deer path. During the winter this was the best part of the day— being set free from that stuffy old room at school.

Before long, Chip came to a rise that gave him a good view. Below, the swiftly moving water of a small river emptied into a lake. Nearby, a tall white pine held a bald eagle's nest.

For a long time, Chip stood without moving, filled with the excitement the huge nest always gave him. Finally his wait was rewarded. High above, two eagles soared against the winter sky.

As he watched, something soared within Chip. "I don't need dumb old school," he thought. "Why should I study that stuff?"

For Chip, school was hard. Sure, he could do the work if he wanted. He just didn't care. Lately he'd been telling himself he didn't care what people thought about him either. But the last time he'd gotten in trouble at school Ma had started crying.

For a moment Chip thought about it, not feeling good. Then he shrugged his shoulders and grinned. "But there's all the things Ma *doesn't* know." Just the same, he still wondered if Rob would snitch on him.

After supper Chip was in his bedroom when Rob's mom came over. Hearing her voice, Chip knew she and Ma were sitting at the kitchen table, drinking coffee. Usually they were good friends. Yet the last few months there'd been trouble between them—trouble Chip had caused.

Quietly he opened his door a crack and listened. Now and then he picked out his name and some words—playground, principal, trouble.

"Today I missed a can of gas," said Rob's mom, her voice a bit louder. "I asked Rob about it, and he said. . . ."

Ma's answer sounded angry. "How do you know Rob's telling the truth?"

For a moment there was an awful quiet. Then Rob's mom broke the stillness, her voice coming clear and cold. "Your kid will never amount to anything."

Chip stepped back away from the door. Anger boiled up within him. He clenched his fists, wanting to fly out of the room and yell at Rob's mom. "That old lady telling my ma a thing like that!" As the hot blood poured through Chip, there was nothing he wanted more than a rip-roaring fight.

"I'll get even with that jerk Rob!" he thought. "He'll never snitch on me again!"

But then Chip had an awful thought. "What if Rob's ma is right? What if I *don't* amount to anything?"

Chip slid to the floor and sat there. Soon he heard Rob's mom get up and leave. Still he sat on the floor, the room dark around him.

"Maybe she's right," thought Chip. Like a large-screen video, pictures seemed to flash in front of him. All the times he'd gotten in trouble. All the times he'd gotten caught. And all the times he'd done something wrong and gotten away with it. For a long time Chip sat there, just thinking.

The next afternoon on the way home from school, Chip swung past the eagles' nest again. As he watched, one of the eagles swooped down, a small branch in his large yellow beak. Chip waited, and before long the other eagle returned. They were adding new twigs to the nest.

Chip felt something stir within him, something that wanted to soar as the eagles did. For the first time in many months he felt hope. "I'm gonna prove Rob's ma is wrong," he promised himself. "I'm gonna make something of myself!"

That afternoon Chip returned the can of gas. Rob's mom looked surprised, but she just said thanks.

The next morning, Chip began listening in class.

He'd looked out the window for so long that it was hard work. Often he didn't feel like trying, but then he remembered the eagles. As the days went on, he began to understand more of what the teacher said.

It was hardest to stop fighting. The kids at school still looked for reasons to poke fun at him. Often Chip clenched his fists, wanting to beat someone up.

But he and Rob were friends again, and Rob told him, "Just pretend you don't see what they're doing." After that, Chip started getting along with the kids on the playground.

One day he had a thought he wouldn't tell even Rob. "Maybe it's good Rob's ma said what she did." Chip had to admit things were going better.

Off and on Chip watched the eagles from a distance. One morning in May he knew the babies had hatched. The adult eagles flew back and forth, carrying fish and other food in their beaks.

"I better get Rob," Chip thought. "He'll wanna see 'em." It felt good to be buddies again.

Around Chip the woods had come alive with the sounds of spring. Inside, he felt himself stretching up, up, up. In his own way he would soar.

TO TALK ABOUT

▶ How did the kids at school treat Chip? How did he feel about himself?

▶When Chip got in trouble, how did it affect his relationship with Rob? How did it affect the relationship between the two mothers?

▶How is it possible to both like and dislike a person?

▶It would be easy for Chip to think, "Nobody likes me. People have been so mean to me I'm gonna give up." Instead, what was the turning point in Chip's life?

▶How did that turning point make a change in Chip's thinking and behavior? Why was it hard for him to change?

▶What hard things have happened to you? How did you react to those hard things?

▶When Chip started to change, he began using all the ability God had given him. In what ways would you like to grow and use all of your ability? In what ways can the Holy Spirit give you the power to change?

The LORD said, "I carried you on eagles' wings and brought you to myself." (Exodus 19:4)

Help me, Jesus, to be honest with myself about where I'm at. Thank You that if I'm honest, You can turn the hard things in my life into something good. Give me the Holy Spirit's power to help me become the person You want me to be.

YOU ARE LOVED!

Do you remember Jenny and Eric and how they felt? They were thinking, "I want to be liked. I want people cheering for me. I want them to make me feel like they think I'm the greatest kid on earth."

While reading these stories, you met kids who felt the same way. You made choices. Or you thought about ones you'd like to make.

Perhaps you also made a discovery. Jesus loves you, whoever you are, whatever has happened to you. Whatever you face, you can count on Him.

But there's a choice to make. *Do you want to receive His help?*

When you say YES! you live under God's protec-

175

tion. You let Him give you the power and the help you need.

Maybe you've discovered it's easier to trust Jesus when it's rough going. It's easier because you can no longer depend on yourself.

That's a good place to be.

That's when you learn to know God. And your relationship with Him is the most important relationship of all.

The book of Daniel says, "The people who know their God shall be strong and do great things" (Daniel 11:32, TLB).

Do you want to be strong in God? Do you want to do great things for Him? Not to make yourself look good, but because you love Him?

The great things of God happen when you choose, like Daniel, to put God first. Then your other relationships fall into place. Your friendships become real and lasting and fun.

Sometimes you may feel, "The choices are so hard I'm afraid to make any at all." In those times, ask Jesus to show you what to do. Then be willing to do it.

Other times you may think, "Oops! I goofed!" When that happens, be honest with Jesus. Tell Him about it. Then ask Him to help you turn your goofs into something good. All of us learn, not only by our good choices, but also through our poor ones.

The great things of God begin in small ways, with

day-by-day choices. The small choices you make add up to big ones. The small choices form the pattern of your life. But they also help you when it comes time to make big choices.

So keep on making good choices in whatever is in front of you each day. Keep on choosing your friends. Keep on choosing to be a friend to your family and others.

Most of all, choose to know God. Choose to put Him first.

Then you'll remember that Jesus always stands with His arms open to you. He's cheering for you. He wants the best for you. He wants you to know, *"I have called you friends. . . . As the Father has loved me, so have I loved you. Now remain in my love"* (John 15:15 and 9).